Confrontation at Worms

Confrontation at Worms

Martin Luther and the Diet of Worms

De Lamar Jensen

With a complete
English translation of the
Edict of Worms

Library of Congress Cataloging in Publication Data

Jensen, De Lamar, 1925-
    Confrontation at Worms.

    (Friends of the Brigham Young University Library keepsake series, no. 6)
    The Edict is translated from the copy in the J. Reuben Clark, Jr., Library at
Brigham Young University, "a French version published in Paris, apparently by
the printer Pierre Gromors."
    Includes bibliographical references.
    1. Luther, Martin, 1483-1546. 2. Worms, Diet of, 1521. I. Holy Roman Empire.
Laws, statutes, etc., 1519-1556 (Charles V). Edict of Worms. English. 1973. II.
Title. III. Series: Brigham Young University, Provo, Utah. Library. Friends.
Keepsake series, no. 6.
BR326.6.J45   284'.1'0924 [B]   73-5906
ISBN 0-8425-0286-6

Brigham Young University Press, Provo, Utah 84602
©1973 by Brigham Young University Press. All rights reserved
Printed in the United States of America
73 1.5M 11259

Contents

Brigham Young University Press
Published in conjunction with
J. Reuben Clark, Jr., Library
Provo, Utah

Cover: Luther as the "German Hercules." A woodcut by Hans Holbein the Younger.
Frontispiece: cast lead medallion of Luther taken from the Lucas Cranach engraving of 1521 and bearing the inscription (struck at a later date), "If Luther's heresy is proven, then the Lord Christ is also a heretic".

To My Father-in-Law
Dr. Edgar H. White

Introduction

n our present world of machines and computers, a world growing more impersonal by the day, we sometimes despair at the apparent insignificance of man and the ineffectiveness of human endeavor against the onrush of history. And yet, although it is impossible for individuals to determine their milieu entirely, or difficult to control even in minor ways the course of events, it is human beings, if not singly, at least in concert, who create the situations and the instruments of change that in turn overrun us. The origin of even the most involved and complex electronic device was a human mind, or many minds, motivated by millions of human desires and intentions, challenged and further stimulated by difficulties and obstacles, both human and natural, and pervaded throughout by the spark of divine inspiration. The course of human history is shaped by human beings, even though we are not always able to recognize the nature and direction of their impact.

In the simpler world of the sixteenth century it was less difficult to see the immediate effects of human influence on affairs, especially when that influence was exercised through the clash of opposing ideas and personalities. The document presented here — a recent and valuable acquisition by the J. Reuben Clark, Jr., Library — came into being as a result of such an encounter. The Edict of Worms vividly testifies to the power and intensity of the mounting religious struggle that reached its first great climax in April 1521 in the confrontation at Worms between Martin Luther and Emperor Charles V. The effects of that confrontation were immediate, and its ramifications have profoundly influenced the world to the present time. Yet the irreparable split in Christendom which resulted from that growing conflict of ideas, faith, and personality has its origin in a rather simple concept of divine righteousness and human need. The path from Wittenberg to Worms, from universal Catholicism to fragmented Protestantism, was a series of conflicts and confrontations pitting Martin Luther first against himself, then against the clergy and the papacy, and finally against the empire.

Luther's Conflict with Himself

artin Luther was a religious man. From earliest boyhood he was sensitively aware of the ravages of sin in the world and was deeply concerned about his relationship to God and about the fate of his soul. Throughout the Holy Roman Empire, and particularly in the regions of central Germany where Luther was born and reared, religious restlessness was much in evidence. People were anxiously trying to express their deep religious feelings and to receive the personal satisfaction of those expressions. Participation in religious sacraments and ceremonies — the mass, pilgrimages, indulgences, charities, relic and saint worship, Mariolatry — reached a high point in the early sixteenth century. One reason for the fervor of these devotions was the belief in the imminence of the second coming of the Savior, an advent which was expected to take place in the fullness of divine power and glory. In this way eschatology combined with unrequited devotions, social frustrations, and the constant harassment of supposed witches, demons, and evil spirits to give a great urgency to religious expressions.

Like his contemporaries, young Luther was influenced by demonology and by fear of the sudden coming of the Lord. From an early age he was also an avid reader of the Bible and had an unusually keen interest in theological matters. His conception of the Savior was a mixture of simple faith in Christ the protector and fear of Christ the judge and stern avenger. Luther's childhood anxiety over the Last Judgment was intensified by belief in its nearness. Only the assurance of the compassionate intervention of the Virgin Mother — and a galaxy of other saints and patrons — relieved the consuming fear of divine judgment. It was in part this gnawing apprehension and doubt about his ability ever to do all the things God required of him if he remained in the world that prompted Luther to abandon the study of law and turn to the monastery when he was twenty-one.

Even within the quiet safety of the cloister Luther failed to find peace. Throwing himself into the monotonous routine of monastic life with enthusiasm

Luther as a young man. Drawing by Siegfried Reinhardt for the Fourth International Congress of Luther Research, August 1971.

and uncompromising devotion during his novitiate, he was a model monk. And yet his soul was tormented by fears and doubts. Living as pure and strict a life as was humanly possible still failed to bring the assurance of divine acceptance. Martin remained painfully aware of his sins and frighteningly conscious of the chasm separating him from God. Thirty years later he wrote of his monastic experience: "Though I lived as a monk without reproach, I felt that I was a sinner before God with an extremely disturbed conscience."[1] Even his return to scholarly studies — recommended by his vicar and friend, Johann von Staupitz — and his subsequent achievement of the doctorate in biblical theology did not relieve his conscience nor answer his questions. Could God be just or kind or merciful when he required more of man than any human could possibly achieve? Such thoughts creeping continually into Luther's tormented mind gave him even greater anxiety. For how could he love a God whose righteousness consisted of faultlessly judging the unrighteousness of men? Later Luther reminisced: "I did not love — indeed, I hated — this just God who punished sinners."[2]

At the heart of his dilemma was Luther's conception of the "justice of God" (*Iustitia Dei*) as punitive, retributive justice, by which the Lord weighs merit (good works) against sins (bad works) and makes eternal judgments according to the balance of the two. Luther had been taught this notion at home and had had it reinforced both by the rigors of monastic discipline and by his study of scholastic theology. As long as he continued to conceive of *Iustitia* in this punitive sense, Luther's internal struggle continued.

It is impossible to say with certainty just when he began to interpret *Iustitia* in another way and there-

---

1. *D. Martin Luthers Werke,* Kritische Gesamtausgabe, 98 vols. to date (Weimar: Hermann Böhlaus Nachfolger, 1883–), 54:185; commonly known as *Weimarer Ausgabe* and hereafter cited *WA.* Cf. Helmut T. Lehmann, ed., *Luther's Works,* 44 vols. to date (Philadelphia: Fortress Press; St. Louis: Concordia Publishing House, 1955–), 34:336; hereafter cited *LW.*

2. *WA,* 54:185; *LW,* 34:336-37. See the lucid description of Luther's struggle in Gordon Rupp, *Luther's Progress to the Diet of Worms, 1521* (New York: Harper & Row, 1964), pp. 26-35.

by to initiate the theological revolution that would overturn the entire Roman church. It took place sometime between 1512, when he received the doctorate, and 1519, as he prepared his second course of Wittenberg lectures on Galatians. The transformation probably did not occur before 1514 and was well under way by 1517, when the indulgence controversy catapulted him into the spotlight. The so-called tower experience, whether it was a sudden revelation or a gradual realization, was the crucial turning point in Luther's life. In his preface to the first collected edition of his Latin writings (1545), Luther recalled in this way the occasion of his coming into a new understanding of Romans 1:17:

Through God's mercy, as I meditated day and night, pondering the connections of the words (namely, "The justice of God is revealed," as it is written, and "The Just shall live by faith."), at last I began to understand that the justice of God is that free gift of God (i.e., faith) by which the just man lives. Therefore, this sentence, "The justice of God is revealed in the gospel," should be understood in a passive sense as that [gift] whereby a merciful God justifies us through faith, as it is written: "The just shall live by faith." At this I felt as though I had been born again and had entered through open gates into paradise itself. From here the whole face of the Scriptures was altered. I ran through the Scriptures as memory served and collected the same analogy in other words, such as "the work of God" (opus Dei), that is, that which God works in us; "the power of God" (virtus Dei), that with which he makes us strong; "the wisdom of God" (sapientia Dei), in which he makes us wise; "the strength of God" (fortitudo Dei), "the salvation of God" (salus Dei), and "the glory of God" (gloria Dei).

Whereas formerly I had hated the words "justice of God," now I loved and extolled them as the sweetest of all words, and that place in Paul was for me as the gate to paradise.[3]

Thus Luther came to believe that the justice of God was really the *righteousness* of God, by which he bestows faith, and thereby salvation, upon man through Jesus Christ. Luther had rediscovered grace — or reinterpreted it at least. *Iustitia Dei* has nothing to do with rewarding good deeds and punishing bad ones, he concluded. Salvation is not *earned* by men but rather *given* by God. Its prerequisite is

---

3. *WA*, 54:186; *LW*, 34:337.

faith alone (*sola fides*), and that is granted by God's grace. Man can never merit salvation; it comes by grace alone (*sola gratia*). Here was the core of Luther's theology and the central feature of Protestantism, to which it gave birth. Good works, therefore, whether they are moral or sacramental, cannot make good men. But good men always produce good works.

In a single stroke Luther's simple reinterpretation of scripture altered the whole thrust of his theological development. His *kampf* with himself now carried him to struggle with others. It is easy for us to see the implications of Luther's thought. If men do not need sacramental works to gain merit toward salvation, they do not need sacraments; without sacraments there is no need for priests; without priests . . . and so on, until the entire sacramental system of the church, including the papal curia and the pope himself, can be dispensed with. As far as salvation is concerned, said Luther, "every man is his own priest."

Surprisingly, Luther did not reach these conclusions overnight. He seemed content to continue performing his academic duties at the new University of Wittenberg (founded by Elector Frederick of Saxony in 1502) as a lecturer in sacred scripture, occupying the Chair of Biblical Theology, and to carry out his ecclesiastical responsibilities as subprior of Wittenberg and district vicar of eleven convent cloisters in the surrounding area — all without paying much attention to higher authorities of the church. Perhaps he was so relieved by the resolution of his inner turmoil that he had no desire to carry the attack further. Luther was a hard-working and outspoken teacher and pastor, but he was not a revolutionary. He did not intend to found a new church. For him there was only one gospel, the gospel of Christ. His revolt was forced upon him by the rigidity of the ecclesiastical system of which he was a part, by the dogmatic narrowness of rival clerics, by the revolutionary implications of his new theology, and by his own stubborn refusal to compromise. It was marked by mounting rounds of contention and conflict.

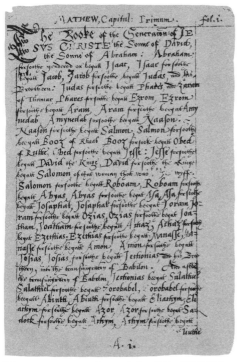

Manuscript version of the Wyclif Bible.

Contention with the Clergy

uther's "Gospel of the Cross" gradually drew him into contention with many spokesmen of the Roman church, official and unofficial. The most frequently abused practice in the church was penance, that sacrament by which the temporal penalty of sin was remitted in absolution. Many shortcuts to that remission had been devised by Luther's time, and one of these was the indulgence. Indulgences, which in the early Christian church were public "satisfactions" (almsgiving, fasting, etc.) imposed by the congregation in order for the penitent to regain full fellowship, had degenerated into a method of remitting the guilt as well as the temporal penalty for sin through the purchase of papal "letters of credit" drawing upon the treasury of merit (*Thesaurus Meritorum*) built up by the surplus good works of Christ and the saints. Indulgences gradually developed into a lucrative and necessary adjunct to the papal financial machinery. They became even more flagrantly pecuniary and theologically questionable with the issuing of special indulgences to raise revenue for specific projects, and plenary indulgences, granting coverage in full for all sins. In 1476 Pope Sixtus IV gave indulgences their final travesty by granting their vicarious application to the dead souls in purgatory. Many theologians were embarrassed by this decision because it was indefensible in canon law. Nevertheless, the indulgence traffic flourished, becoming a major church business by the early sixteenth century.

The indulgence trade impinged upon political affairs as well. When Albrecht of Brandenburg aspired to the influential archbishopric of Mainz (even though he had already been granted the sees of Magdeburg and Halberstadt and was, therefore, not entitled to another benefice), he persuaded Pope Leo X to grant him the benefice for 10,000 ducats in addition to the usual 12,000 ducats fee. Albrecht borrowed from the Fugger bankers of Augsburg to pay these huge sums, and the pope agreed to help facilitate repayment by authorizing the sale of a special plenary indulgence (supposedly for the building of Saint Peter's in Rome) in Albrecht's lands and

Indulgence sales in the early sixteenth century. So lucrative was the "holy trade," according to this woodcut by Jörg Breu the Elder, that the coffers were filled with money minted on the spot. The papal authorization for the sale is attached to a pole in the form of a cross.

The indulgence trade. Detail from a woodcut by Hans Holbein the Younger. Pope Leo is shown handing a letter of indulgence to a Dominican friar. On the left indulgences are being dispensed to those who can afford to buy them, while a beggar is being turned away. On the right a church official is directing a kneeling man to the contribution chest into which the widow is placing her mite.

in those of his brother, Margrave Joachim, elector of Brandenburg. One-half of the income from this indulgence would go directly to Rome and the other half to the Fuggers until the debt to them was paid.

When the enthusiastic Dominican friar, Johann Tetzel, came hawking this new indulgence through nearby Brandenburg, Luther could tolerate the outrage no longer. "I'll knock a hole in his drum," was the Wittenberger's immediate reaction. Later he observed, "I was completely dead to the world until God deemed that the time had come; then Junker Tetzel excited me with indulgences, and Dr. Staupitz spurred me on against the pope."[4] Seeing that indulgences mitigated true repentance by relieving the purchaser of all necessity for contrition and sorrow, Luther challenged the Dominicans, who were the leaders of the "holy trade" in indulgences, to academic disputation. This was a time-honored method of investigating ecclesiastical disputes and exposing theological errors. Luther made his challenge in the form of a written proposition consisting of ninety-five rather disorganized aphorisms or talking points against indulgences and related matters, which he posted on the door of the castle church in Wittenberg on the eve of All Saints' Day, 1517.[5]

In the Ninety-Five Theses, Luther particularly sounded the note of resentment against Roman exploitation of German freedoms, against the pope's implied jurisdiction over purgatory, and against the unhealthy attitude and dangerous state of mind produced by the sale and purchase of indulgences. There was nothing strange or unusual in Luther's action, except that he indicated his intention to en-

---

4. *D. Martin Luthers Werke: Tischreden* [Table Talk], 4, no. 4707; hereafter cited *Tischreden*. Two very different but both excellent examinations of Luther's role in the indulgence controversy may be found in James Atkinson, *Martin Luther and the Birth of Protestantism* (Harmondsworth: Penguin Books, 1968), pp. 141–56, and R. H. Fife, *The Revolt of Martin Luther* (New York: Columbia University Press, 1957), pp. 245–71.

5. The actuality of this event has recently been brought into question by Erwin Iserloh in an essay entitled *Luther zwischen Reform und Reformation: Der Thesenanschlag fand nicht statt* [Münster: Verlag Aschendorff, 1966], trans. Jared Wicks, S. J., (Boston: Beacon Press, 1968). His evidence is circumstantial and highly speculative, however, and does not offset Melanchthon's testimony that the theses were in fact posted.

Cardinal Albrecht of Brandenburg, bishop of Halberstadt, archbishop of Magdeburg, archbishop and elector of Mainz, brother to Joachim, elector of Brandenburg. Engraving by Albrecht Dürer.

gage in the debate himself rather than to advance one of his students. But the situation was unique. First, the issue appears to have been of greater public interest than even Luther had suspected; and second, through the miracle of the printing press, the arguments raised by Luther were soon being circulated throughout Germany and beyond. Reactions to the theses varied. Friends and sympathizers praised the work but feared for Luther's safety, and foes attacked it as either irrelevant or blasphemous. But no one saw in it the opening declaration of the Reformation.

Johannes Tezelius Dominicaner Müuch/ mit seinen Römischen Ablaßkram/ welchen er im Jahr Christi 1517. in Deutschenlanden zu marckt gebracht/ wie er in der Kirchen zu Pirn in seinem Vaterland abgemahlet ist.

O ihr deutschen mercket mich recht/
   Des heiligen Vaters Papstes Knecht/
Bin ich/ vnd er in euch jtzt allein/
   Zehn tausent vnd neun hundert carein/
Gnad vnd Ablaß von einer Sünd/
   Vor euch/ ewer Eltern/ Weib vnd Kind/
Sol ein jeder gewehret sein
   So viel ihr legt ins Kästelein/
So bald der Gülden im Becken klingt/
   Im huy die Seel im Himel springt/

Caricature of Johann Tetzel's indulgence selling.

When he saw how widely the theses were circulating, Luther composed a more formal elucidation, clarifying them in many points and buttressing them with scriptural documentation. This publication, *Explanations of the Disputation Concerning the Value of Indulgences,* with a special dedicatory letter to Pope Leo X, served as a defense against the mounting attacks of his opponents. Even before the completion of this work, Luther had published in German a *Sermon on Indulgence and Grace* strongly condemning the claim of the hawkers that indul-

13

The castle church in Wittenberg. Woodcut by Lucas Cranach from the *Wittenberger Heiligthums Buch.*

gences could release souls from purgatory and denouncing his defamers as "blockheads who have never even smelled the Bible or read a word of Christian doctrine."[6] The coarse and aggressive tone of Luther's speech and writing quickly earned him more enemies. The Dominicans, especially, took the stump against this upstart monk. From Frankfurt came sharp attacks by Wimpina and Tetzel; from Cologne came criticism from Jakob Hochstraten; from Dresden sounded the hostile murmurings of Hieronymus Emser; from Ingolstadt rose the *Obelisks* of Johann Eck; and from Rome echoed the

6. *WA,* 1:246; Fife, p. 263.

theological sputterings of Sylvester Prierias and the bishop of Ascoli.

Although many in his own Augustinian order were alarmed by Luther's writings, they had no intention of abandoning him to the Dominicans. In April 1518, responding to the invitation of Johann von Staupitz, now vicar-general of all German cloisters of the Congregation of Reformed Augustinians, Luther journeyed to Heidelberg to present his "Wittenberg theology" to the general chapter.[7] The Heidelberg Disputation was a personal victory for Luther and won him a number of friends, including the later Strasbourg reformer, Martin Bucer. Nevertheless, the clouds of opposition were growing heavier around the Wittenberg professor.

As a result both of biased reporting to Rome of some of Luther's vehement sermons and of a forged treatise accredited to Luther, Cardinal Cajetan, then in Augsburg as papal legate to the imperial diet, was instructed to demand Luther's arrest and order him to appear in Rome to answer charges of heresy. Luther was first approached by Cajetan's attendant, who urged Luther to save himself by uttering the one word that would terminate the proceedings: *Revoco* ("I recant"). Luther replied that he would be most willing to say it if he were convinced that he was in error.[8] Cajetan was a kindly pastor and hoped to persuade Luther by fatherly counsel to cease his attacks on the doctrines and practices of the church. But the cardinal's orders were specifically to demand unconditional recantation from Luther for all of his writings. Luther would not listen to such a demand. He wanted to be heard; he wanted to debate the issues with other learned doctors of theology and to be judged by an impartial tribunal on the basis of the arguments. He adamantly refused to recant, and the Augsburg interview ended in failure for both sides. Now Luther was even more convinced of the insincerity and duplicity of the

Johannes Tetzel von Leipzig
SS. Theol. Doctor und Professor, ein Bruder
des Dominicaner Ordens, Ketzer Meister, und
Papstlicher Gnädenprediger, oder Ablas Crämer.

Brühl fe. Lips.

---

7. *LW*, 31:35–70.

8. *Tischreden*, no. 3857, 3:661–63; *LW*, 57:285; *D. Martin Luthers Werke: Briefwechsel*, 1:209–10, Luther to Spalatin, 10 October 1518; hereafter cited as *Briefwechsel*. On the proceedings at Augsburg see *LW*, 31:253–92; and E. G. Schweibert, *Luther and His Times* (St. Louis: Concordia Publishing House, 1950), pp. 338–57.

clergy, while the curia became satisfied that Luther was a rebellious and obstinate heretic. Cajetan had no alternative other than to condemn "the shabby little friar" and order his appearance in Rome.

However, the political situation in the winter of 1518–19 called for more circumspection than was recommended by the cardinal legate. Frederick, "the Wise," elector of Saxony, was reluctant to surrender his valuable subject to the dangers of a Roman court. He recalled the fate of John Hus just one hundred years earlier. Besides, Luther was a much more valuable political weapon alive than dead. Thus, instead of submitting Luther to the pope, Frederick sent testimonials in Luther's behalf from the Wittenberg faculty together with a letter excusing Luther from traveling to Rome on account of his health and "the perils of the way." Under the circumstances Pope Leo was not likely to press Frederick too far: Emperor Maximilian I was in poor health, and the pope, not favoring Maximilian's choice of his grandson, King Charles I of Spain, as his successor, hoped to convince Frederick to use his influence as an imperial elector to prevent Charles's election. The Luther situation had to be treated with caution.

In November, Karl von Miltitz, chamberlain of the pope's household, was dispatched to Saxony to present the Golden Rose (the highest recognition given for service to Christendom and loyalty to the papacy) to Frederick for his prominence in promoting peace and understanding. Miltitz also carried with him a decree concerning "a certain monk in Germany" who was making erroneous interpretations of scripture and false charges against the curia. Being a Saxon himself, and knowing that he would receive the accolades of both church and state if he were to solve the thorny Lutheran problem, Miltitz aspired to effect a reconciliation between Luther and the pope. After having summarily reprimanded Tetzel for his indulgence errors, the papal courier cum diplomat met Luther at Altenburg on 5 and 6 January 1519 and exercised all his diplomacy, assuring his countryman that he had been misunderstood and misquoted in Rome and guaranteeing him amnesty and favor if he would cease his written and

Luther before Cardinal Cajetan at Augsburg. From a contemporary book illustration.

Frederick, "the Wise," elector of Saxony and Luther's patron. Engraving by Albrecht Dürer.

oral assaults on the church. Luther denied ever attacking the church and agreed to withhold further polemics if he were not slandered by others.[9]

But the tranquility of January and February was merely the calm before the storm. The flood of acrimonious writings did not subside. Of the many theologians (and nontheologians) with whom Luther exchanged verbal volleys, none had so irritated and exacerbated him as the talented and outspoken Ingolstadt professor, Johann Eck, whom Luther referred to as a "deceitful man" and "that little glory-hungry beast."[10] Early in 1519 a debate was arranged between Eck and Luther's associate, Andreas Carlstadt. Luther was green with envy, for it was with him, not Carlstadt, that Eck had disputed, and this was exactly the kind of public hearing Luther desperately wanted. Finally achieving permission to participate in the disputation, Luther entered the lists on July 4.

The Leipzig professor of Greek, Peter Mosellanus, described the contestants in the following manner:

Martin is of middle height, emaciated from care and study, so that you can almost count his bones through his skin. He is in the vigor of manhood [however] and has a clear, penetrating voice. He is learned and has the Scripture at his fingers' ends. He knows Greek and Hebrew sufficiently to judge of the interpretations. A perfect forest of words and ideas stands at his command. He is affable and friendly, in no sense dour or arrogant. He is equal to anything. In company he is vivacious, jocose, always cheerful and gay no matter how hard his adversaries press him. Everyone chides him for the fault of being a little too insolent in his reproaches and more caustic than is prudent for an innovator in religion or becoming to a theologian. Much the same can be said of Carlstadt, though in a lesser degree. He is smaller than Luther, with a complexion of smoked herring. His voice is thick and unpleasant. He is slower in memory and quicker in anger. Eck is a heavy, square-set fellow with a full German voice supported by a hefty chest. He would make a tragedian or town crier, but his voice is rather rough than clear. His eyes and mouth and his whole face remind one more of a butcher than a theologian. [Mosellanus

9. *Briefwechsel,* 1:289–91; *Luther's Works: Letters,* 48:97–100, Luther to Elector Frederick.

10. *Briefwechsel,* 1:325, 344–45, Luther to Spalatin, Luther to Staupitz.

further noted that Eck] *has a fine memory; were his understanding only equal to it he would possess all nature's gifts.*[11]

The Leipzig debate was the most important landmark on Luther's road to Worms.[12] Eck was an experienced and clever debator as well as a man of considerable scholarly attainments, having become a lecturer at Freiburg at 16, dean of liberal arts at 22, and rector of the University of Ingolstadt at 26. Not as versed in the scriptures nor as exuberant in argument as was Luther, he nevertheless knew what he was doing and proceeded in his prosecution with masterful skill. Luther was particularly prepared to debate indulgences, but Eck wisely skirted this issue because he knew Luther was on firm ground. Tetzel *had* exceeded his commission and Eck was not inclined to put himself in the awkward position of defending him. Rather, he maneuvered Luther into a corner by cleverly drawing out of him more dogmatic statements of belief — particularly with regard to papal and conciliar authority — than he had hitherto expressed. He also associated Luther's ideas with the hated Hussites, whom everyone, including Luther, considered heretics. When Eck tricked him into asserting that many of Hus's articles condemned by the church were both Christian and evangelical, Duke George was heard to sputter a loud curse.

The central issue of the Leipzig debate was authority: where, by whom, and how it was exercised. Luther accepted the church, the catholic church, the universal church of God, but he refused to equate this with the church of Rome. According to scripture, he insisted, the only head of the church is

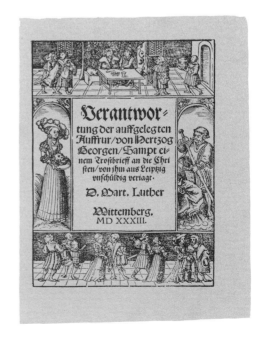

11. Preserved Smith and Charles M. Jacobs, eds., *Luther's Correspondence and Other Contemporary Letters*, 2 vols. (Philadelphia, 1913), 1:257–62, quoted in Roland H. Bainton, *Here I Stand: A Life of Martin Luther* (New York: Abingdon Press, 1950), p. 113, and in Schwiebert, *Luther and His Times*, p. 414. For this and other contemporary reports of the debate see Valentin E. Löscher, *Vollständige Reformations-Acta und Documenta*, 3 vols. (Leipzig, 1720–29), vol. 3, and Johann G. Walch, ed., *D. Martin Luthers Sämtliche Schriften*, 24 vols. (Halle, 1740), vol. 15.

12. *LW*, 31:307–25; Donald J. Ziegler, ed., *Great Debates of the Reformation* [trans. A. K. Stallman from Otto Seitz, ed., *Der authentische Text der Leipziger Disputation* (Berlin: C. A. Schwetschke & Sohn, 1903)] (New York: Random House, 1969), pp. 3–34.

Luther depicted beneath the sign of a dove. Contemporary woodcut.

Christ. Before the week had ended, Luther had affirmed not only that popes could and often did err in matters of doctrine as well as morals but that councils, too, were frequently fallible in that respect.

In the theological sense it cannot be said that there was a winner or a loser in the Leipzig debate — both sides claimed the victory — but in the historical sense it was a decisive event. Not only did it further clarify the issues and delineate the doctrinal problems, it also opened Luther's own eyes to the full implications of his "tower experience." He was now convinced of the chasm that separated him from the majority of churchmen. He was committed to God's truth — a truth contrary to what was being taught by Rome! By Roman standards he *was* a Hussite and heretic; he could see that now. And "so were Paul

Johann Eck, professor of theology at the University of Ingolstadt, Luther's antagonist at the Leipzig Debate. Copper engraving by Peter Weinher the Elder.

and Augustine, word for word," he wrote to his friend, Spalatin, secretary to the Saxon elector.[13]

The Luther issue was not only clarified by the Leipzig debate; it was generalized. Now it was obvious for everyone to see that Luther was not a harmless (even though loud) sniper at minor ecclesiastical vices, or even at clerical corruption altogether. He was in opposition to the entire theological basis of the Roman church. "Others have attacked the life," he is reported to have said. "I attack the doctrine."[14] It was not just the abuses of Roman Catholicism that he objected to — as did Erasmus and the Christian humanists — rather, he attacked Catholicism itself.

13. *Briefwechsel,* 2:42, Luther to Spalatin.
14. Roland H. Bainton, *The Reformation of the Sixteenth Century* (Boston: Beacon Press, 1952), p. 24.

The Leipzig Debate. A nineteenth-century drawing by Gustav König.

*Someone said to me, "What a sin and scandal all these
clerical vices are: the fornication, the drunkenness, the un-
bridled passion for sport!" Yes, I must confess that these are
dreadful scandals, indeed, and they should be denounced
and corrected. But the vices to which you refer are plain
for all to see; they are grossly material; everyone perceives
them, and so everyone is stirred to anger by them. Alas,
the real evil, the incomparably more baneful and cruel
canker, is the deliberate silence regarding the word of
Truth, or else its adulteration. Yet who feels the horror
of this?*[15]

———
15. Henri Daniel-Rops, *The Protestant Reformation*, Trans.
Audrey Butler (New York: E. P. Dutton & Co., 1961), p. 299.

Contemporary pamphlet on the Leipzig Debate in 1519.

Luther had no desire to effect an ecclesiastical upheaval, much less a social, economic, or political revolution. His war was theological. He was fighting in behalf of "Truth" against the tyranny of error. And as the champion of truth he was unwilling and unable to compromise in the least. It is one of the paradoxes of the Reformation that his simple message contained many additional implications and that most of his followers rallied to his banner for reasons tangential to Luther's theological motives.

Collision with the Pope

ollowing Leipzig, Luther busied himself with an outpouring of theological and polemical writings that was amazing in view of his continuing responsibilities as professor and priest. During the autumn and winter of 1519–20 he completed his commentary on Psalms, composed a small book to comfort Frederick of Saxony (who was ill), began a book of sermons, and wrote a great number of tracts on a variety of topics from prayer and sacraments to blasphemy and usury. He also wrote a major treatise, *On Good Works*, reemphasizing the primacy of faith and its transformation into good works. At the same time he produced a book on the mass, which he called *A Sermon on the New Testament*, and another, *On the Manner of Confession*, while pouring out a steady barrage of letters to both friend and foe. His output was prodigious. In December he confessed to Spalatin that he was doing the work of four men: "The Psalter requires a whole man; the series of sermons — for which I am working through the Gospels and Genesis — a whole man; the prayers and services of my order, a third man; and the work of exegesis, a fourth — to say nothing of my letter writing and my occupation with the affairs of other people, including the meeting with good friends."[16] Yet all of this Luther took in stride, being a facile writer, "swift of hand and quick in memory."[17] In this growing body of writings it is obvious that Luther had a clearer conception of his position in relation to the church than he had had before the Leipzig debate. Now he was forced to accept the implications of his stand.

To many of his opponents, Luther's disrespectful and vulgar attitude toward the pope, and papal authority in general, was his most reprehensible trait as well as his most vulnerable mistake. The appearance in May 1520 of a book staunchly defending papal power, written by an excited Leipzig Franciscan, Augustin von Alveld,[18] aroused Luther's in-

---

16. *Briefwechsel*, 1:594–95.
17. *Briefwechsel*, 2:36, Luther to Spalatin, 8 February 1520.

Martin Luther in 1520. Woodcut by Lucas Cranach.

Pope Leo X. Detail of an engraving from the painting by Raphael located in the Pitti Palace, Florence.

Luther cartoon of 1521 caricaturing five of Luther's most agressive opponents: Dr. Thomas Murner, the Alsace cat; Dr. Hieronymus Emser, the Leipzig goat; Pope Leo X, the Antichrist lion; Dr. Johann Eck, the Ingolstadt pig; and Dr. Lemp, the Tübingen dog.

dignation. Immediately he responded with a vernacular pamphlet, *On the Papacy at Rome,* denouncing the usurpations of the papal curia and strongly denying the traditional identification of the church of God with the church of Rome. Gone were the conciliatory words with which he had addressed the pope just a year and one-half earlier.[19] Now the bleating of the little sheep had become the roaring of an aroused lion declaring, "Christ cannot have a

18. Augustin von Alfeld (or Alvelt), a young lecturer of the Franciscan convent at Leipzig, was the first and one of the few Franciscans to attack Luther. *See* Leonhard Lemmens, "Pater Augustin von Alfeld," *Erläuterungen und Ergänzungen zu Janssens Geschichte des deutschen Volks* (Freiburg, 1899), 1, as cited in Fife, pp. 499–500.

19. *Briefwechsel,* 1:292, Luther to Pope Leo X, 5 or 6 January 1519. Luther pleaded with the pope to be gracious and condescend to lend his ears in a fatherly way and "listen to the bleating of this, your little sheep, for you truly stand in the place of Christ."

vicar in his church. That is why neither pope nor bishop can ever become Christ's vicar or regent."[20] "Let the pope be the pope" if he likes, Luther raved, but "I shall accept what the pope establishes and does only on condition that I judge it first on the basis of Holy Scripture."[21] Later, in response to Prierias's attack on this work, Luther wrote vehemently, "If we punish thieves with the *furca* [a two-pronged instrument of sixteenth-century punishment], brigands with the sword, and heretics with fire, why don't we rather take these miserable monsters — these cardinals, these popes, and the whole swarm of Roman Sodomites who corrupt the youth and the church of God — and put them to the sword and wash our hands in their blood?"[22]

During the summer and autumn of 1520 Luther composed his three famous treatises which, taken together, summarize the nature and extent of his break with Rome. The first of these was the strongly worded German call to arms against the papal enemy. Now it was clear to Luther that the papacy would never change its course nor reform and correct its errors, and he called upon the secular rulers of Germany to take the lead in ecclesiastical and moral reform. This *Address to the Christian Nobility of the German Nation for the Reform of the Christian Estate* was the clarion call of the Reformation. It was also the most revolutionary of Luther's writings until that time, for in it he denounced the authority of the pope over secular rulers, denied the papal monopoly on the interpretation of scripture, and decried the pope's assertion of exclusive right to summon a general council. It was also the most effective instru-

Woodcut from a 1521 pamphlet, showing men in a heated religious discussion at left and peasants drinking at the right.

---

20. *WA,* 6:298; *LW,* 39:72.

21. *WA,* 6:322; *LW,* 39:101.

22. *WA,* 6:347. By this time Luther frequently lashed out at his opponents with such crude expressions. He also used contemptuous and animated names to characterize them. He referred to Eck as a viper, called the bishop of Brandenburg a bladder blown up by Eck's wind, addressed Emser as "the goat at Leipzig" and a coarse donkey who knew as much about philosophy and theology "as an ass does about music." He called Emser's friend, Thomas Murner, a fool and a blabbermouth. Emser returned the compliments, referring to Luther as "the ox at Wittenberg." *See WA,* 2:625–54; 7:262–83, 621–88; *Briefwechsel,* 1:513–15; *LW,* 39:105–224, *passim;* Ernst Ludwig Enders, ed., *Luther und Emser: Ihre Streitschriften aus dem Jahre 1521,* 2 vols. (Halle : Niemeyer, 1890–92).

Anti-Catholic cartoons contrasting the life of Christ with that of the Antichrist. In one, Christ is shown driving the money changers from

ment in winning the support of the German people against Rome, for it corresponded with the popular antipapalism already rampant, but undirected, in early sixteenth-century Germany. Luther was probably encouraged by others to write this broadside as a rallying point for the antipapists, and in its strong sociopolitical flavor it was a unique and arousing tract.

This was followed closely by "another little song about Rome and the Romanists," *On the Babylonian Captivity of the Church,* written in vigorous Latin to clergymen and theologians. In the *Address to the Christian Nobility* Luther had battered down the outer walls of papal defense. In the *Babylonian Captivity* he directed a frontal attack on its very center. In

the temple. In the other, the pope sells dispensations, favors, and indulgences. From the 1521 *Passional of Christ and Antichrist.*

this radical book Luther attacked the entire clerical-sacramental system of the Roman church, stripping it of its biblical basis and function. This repudiation of the sacramental system theologically demolished the ecclesiastical structure as well and emphasized his affirmation of the priesthood of all believers.

Finally, he summarized his biblical theology as it had then evolved, in a little book, *On the Freedom of a Christian.* Here Luther declared that the Christian believer is made free by faith, which alone justifies and produces good works. By virtue of this faith the Christian is subject to no one but God; yet, as a result of it, he is the servant of all, through love. It is the most conciliatory of the three treatises, yet its premise is the very heart of the Protestant Reformation.

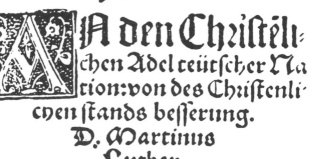
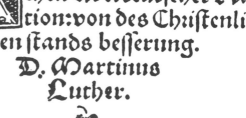

Teütscher Adel. An den Christenlichen Adel teütscher Nation: von des Christenlichen stands besserung. D. Martinus Luther.

wittenberg.

Title page of Luther's *Address to the Christian Nobility of the German Nation*, 1520.

Title page of the German edition of the papal bull, *Exsurge Domine,* 1520.

In the meantime, Pope Leo and the Roman curia had not been idle. Desiring more firsthand information about the Wittenberg monk, Leo summoned Johann Eck to Rome and at the same time renewed Miltitz's commission to Frederick the Wise. Early in 1520 the Roman consistory reopened the case against Luther. A new commission, headed by Cardinal Cajetan, was appointed. Eck was also a member, and his anti-Luther influence more than offset Cajetan's conciliatory disposition.[23] By June 1 the final draft of the bull *Exsurge Domine* ("Arise,

23. Paul Kalkoff, "Die Bulle 'Exsurge'," *Zeitschrift für Kirchengeschichte,* 35(1914):166–203.

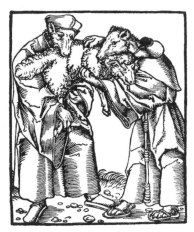

Caricature depicting priest and monk devouring their sheep instead of caring for them.

O Lord'') was completed, and two weeks later it was signed by the papal chancery and publicly proclaimed in the Piazza Navonna. A month later, Eck and Hieronymus Aleander, secretary to the vice-chancellor, departed Rome for Germany officially to present the bull to Luther and to the secular and ecclesiastical authorities in Germany. *Exsurge Domine* was not a bull of excommunication; rather, it was a condemnation, in forty-one articles, of Luther's errors and a threat that if he did not publicly recant and refute these errors within sixty days after receiving the bull, he and his protectors would be under danger of excommunication.

Luther and all Germany knew of the bull long before it was delivered to him on October 10. He was not disturbed in the least. Emboldened by the crescendo of support from thousands of Germans — from peasants to princes — who hated the Roman oppression, Luther made no move toward reconciliation during the sixty days of grace. Instead, he wrote and published a defiant "anti-bull," *Against the Accursed Bull of the Antichrist*, emphatically answering each of the charges against him and adding a few countercharges of his own. And he warned the pope that if the papacy did not radically alter its course, "I and all who worship Christ, will consider your seat possessed by Satan, the damned seat of Antichrist, to which we will neither give obedience nor be subject. Rather, we will detest and execrate it as the main and supreme enemy of Christ."[24] Then on December 10, in a final act of defiance, Luther publicly burned the papal bull and with it a number of previous papal decretals, some of Eck's and Emser's books, and the entire corpus of canon law. There was no turning back now; both Luther and the pope had made that clear. Earlier it might have been possible to assuage the troubled professor by open debate with competent and unprejudiced scholars, pointing out areas of agreement and disagreement in a conciliatory and scholarly manner. At least Luther always maintained that he would have been satisfied had he been heard in- .

24. *WA*, 6:604.

Luther burning the papal bull. Watercolor by C. F. Lessing.

stead of blindly condemned. But the problem was much deeper than he realized. Many social and administrative issues, which he had scarcely seen, were demanding redress. Furthermore, the deep implications of his own doctrinal stand prevented any lasting reconciliation between him and the church. The lines of disagreement were hardened, and the attitude of each side was dogmatic. On 3 January 1521 a bull of excommunication, *Decet Romanum*, announced the pope's final decision.

Confrontation with the Emperor

he political situation of the Holy Roman Empire in 1521 was volatile. German society was in ferment; the growing restlessness of the peasants was echoed both in the disquiet of the cities and in the agitation among noble clans. Economic uncertainty added further stress to already strained political and social relations. Neighboring France, under its flamboyant king, Francis I, was beginning warlike activities that boded no good for the empire. At the same time the ever-threatening Turks were marshalling their giant strength behind the banner of their new sultan, Suleiman, "the Magnificent." But even these external threats failed to draw German society together. Centuries of fragmentation and factionalism had made disorder endemic. Mounting religious tensions further magnified the differences and hatreds between localities, regions, and classes. Luther's disturbance further accelerated this process and added fuel to the longstanding German resentment of Italy and, particularly, of Rome. His attitude and violent words, even more than his spiritual message, caught the imagination and sympathy of the German people.

Into this explosive tinderbox stepped the reserved and untested young Burgundian courtier who had been elected Holy Roman Emperor in June 1519, five months after the death of his grandfather, Maximilian I. Charles V was Flemish by birth and training: he was born in Ghent, and he lived in Flanders and adjacent regions of the Burgundian Netherlands for the first fifteen years of his life. But destiny had not intended that he should be a Diogenes. At age six he inherited all the Burgundian lands that had passed from his grandmother, Mary of Burgundy, to his father, Philip, "the Handsome," who was the son of Maximilian I of Austria. With the death of his father he also became heir to the vast Habsburg territories of central and eastern Europe. Ten years later the dual crowns of Castile and Aragon with their overseas possessions likewise passed to him through his mother, Juana, "*la loca*," and her parents, "the Catholic Kings," Ferdinand and Isabel. So, at age sixteen,

Silver medal of Emperor Charles V, 1521. By an unknown Nürnberg die cutter from a sketch by Albrecht Dürer. Made on the occasion of the Diet of Worms.

Charles of Ghent was titular ruler of more lands in the Old World and in the New than any other European monarch since Charlemagne. But that was not all. In June 1519 this quiet and ungainly youth was elevated to the highest office in Christendom, against the opposition of such political veterans as Francis I, Henry VIII of England, and Pope Leo X. [25]

Inexperienced in the jungle of German politics (although well-tutored in imperial affairs by his

25. The best overall biography of Charles V is still Karl Brandi, *Kaiser Karl V* [trans. C. V. Wedgwood, (London: Jonathon Cape, 1939)] (Munich: F. Bruckmann Verlag, 1937). For a closer look at the emperor's role in the Reformation see Hermann Baumgarten, *Karl V. und die deutsche Reformation,* Schriften des Vereins für Reformationsgeschichte, no. 27, 186 vols. to date (Halle, 1883–). An outstanding recent essay, making the best use of contemporary and modern sources, is H. G. Koenigsberger, "The Empire of Charles V in Europe," in *The New Cambridge Modern History,* ed. G. R. Elton, 14 vols. (Cambridge: Cambridge University Press, 1958), 2:301–33.

The imperial coat of arms of Charles V.

counselors, Chièvres and Chancellor Gattinara, and by his old mentor, Adrian of Utrecht, the future Pope Adrian VI), Charles left Spain, where he had resided since assuming the crowns of Castile and Aragon in 1516, and entered the northern arena. He proceeded to Aachen in October 1520 to receive the traditional crown of the Holy Roman Empire of the German Nation and thence to Worms to preside over his first imperial diet (*Reichstag*).[26] The issues confronting him there were numerous and weighty: a commitment from the German princes for cooperative action against the threatening Turks;

26. On the diet see Paul Kalkoff, *Der Wormser Reichstag von 1521* (Munich: R. Oldenbourg, 1922); Theodor Kolde, *Luther und der Reichstag zu Worms 1521,* Schriften des Vereins für Reformationsgeschichte, no. 1; and especially the recently published anniversary volume edited by Fritz Reuter, *Der Reichstag zu Worms von 1521: Reichspolitik und Luthersache im Auftrag der Stadt Worms zum 450-Jahrgedenken* (Worms: Stadtarchiv Worms, 1971).

preventive measures against the king of France; a possible alliance with England (where Charles's aunt, Catherine of Aragon, was queen); the making of overdue administrative and judicial reforms for the jurisdiction of the empire, particularly the establishment of a council of regency (*Reichsregiment*) to rule during the frequent absences of the emperor; and the creation of a viable financial structure. But the thorniest problem of all was the reform of the church in Germany. Everyone knew it needed reform. Most of the princes felt the papacy had grossly mismanaged its affairs. But who could agree as to what should be changed and how it was to be done?

The seriousness of the religious problem was underlined in the early weeks of the Diet of Worms when the assembled delegates reminded the emperor of the grave disorders in the operation of the church in Germany and suggested that many of Luther's criticisms of the papacy were true and justified. They further urged him to strike at the root of these "oppressive burdens and abuses imposed on and committed against the Empire by the Holy See in Rome."[27] In response to the emperor's request for more specific information about the abuses, a committee submitted a formal and lengthy list of grievances. This remarkable statement itemized and described 102 abuses practiced by Rome or by Roman authority in the ecclesiastical jurisdiction of the German empire.

The pope would need a strong representation at Worms if he hoped to persuade the emperor and diet to support and strengthen his condemnation of Luther. In almost continuous attendance with the emperor before and during the diet were the papal legates, Marino Caracciolo and the wily Hieronymus Aleander, formerly rector of the University of Paris, then Vatican librarian, and now special papal nuncio to Charles V as commissioner for the Luther matter. Unlike Cajetan, Eck, and others who had tried to stem the tide of Lutheran heresy, Aleander was a careful but persistent humanist promoter of papal poli-

---

27. Gerald Strauss, ed., *Manifestations of Discontent in Germany on the Eve of the Reformation: A Collection of Documents* (Bloomington: Indiana University Press, 1971), p. 52.

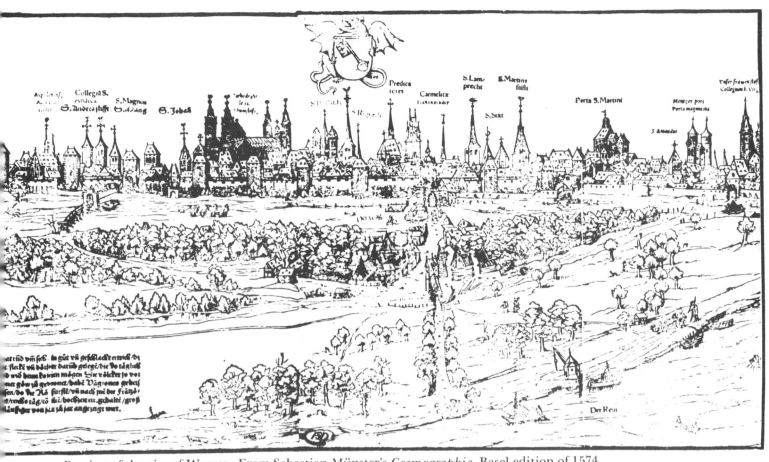

Portion of the city of Worms. From Sebastian Münster's *Cosmographie,* Basel edition of 1574.

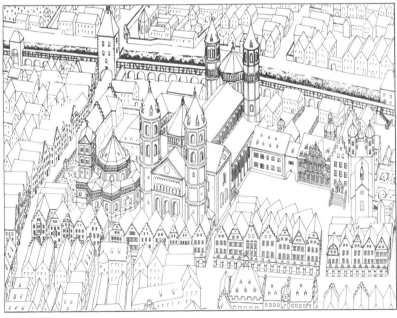

Sketch of the meeting place of the Diet of Worms. Modern reconstruction by Adolf Heiss, 1938, showing the Johanneskirche, the Cathedral, the Bishop's palace, and Stephanskirche.

41

Hieronymus Aleander. Copper engraving by Agostino dei Musi, 1536.

cies. More clearly than many of his colleagues, he saw the dangers implicit in Luther's rebellion, not theological dangers — for Aleander was no theologian — but the larger political implications of the German unrest which was now being channeled and given meaning by Luther's *Address to the German Nobility*. He also discerned, more than other Italians had, the strong antipapal feelings on all levels of German society. Aleander's objective was to obtain an imperial condemnation of Luther in order to give the papal bull support and force in Germany. He was particularly anxious to extract the sentence without allowing Luther another public hearing.[28]

In characteristic manner, the young emperor refused to be crowded into a hasty decision. Besides, he reminded the nuncio, no subject of the imperial crown is ever condemned without a hearing. Somewhat disturbed by Aleander's burning of Luther's books at Louvain in October and at Cologne and Mainz in November, Charles heeded Frederick of Saxony's plea to have Luther brought before a just tribunal. In November he issued an invitation to the elector to bring the controversial Dr. Luther to the Diet of Worms where he would "be heard by learned persons and no wrong be done him."[29] But by the time the imperial session opened on 27 January 1521, Luther's own book-burning orgy and Aleander's persistent pressure had brought the emperor to change his mind about summoning Luther.

Aleander hoped to get the emperor to issue an edict against Luther as quickly as possible, with or without the consent of the Reichstag. For this purpose he had already composed a draft of such an edict before the diet convened in January. Charles V wanted the ban to be issued with the consent of the princes and appointed a commission to look into the matter. Aleander's draft was submitted to the commission and to the Imperial Court Council (*Reichshofrat*), which proceeded to redraft the entire paper. Debate among the princes of the council was intense, almost violent, before they eventually agreed, on February 15, to refer the matter to the whole diet.

On February 19 the diet demanded that Luther be heard before being condemned, and they refused to proceed further with the edict. They recommended that Luther receive a scholarly hearing —

---

28. Adolf Hausrath, *Aleander und Luther auf dem Reichstag zu Worms* (Berlin: G. Grote, 1897); Paul Kalkoff, *Aleander gegen Luther* (Leipzig: Rudolf Haupt, 1908). On Aleander's life see Jules Paquier, *Jérôme Aléandre de sa naissance à la fin de son séjour à Brindes, 1480–1529* (Paris: Ernest Leroux, 1900).

29. Ernst S. Cyprian, "Nützliche Urkunden zur Erläuterung der ersten Reformationsgeschichte," *Tentzels Historischer Bericht vom Anfang und Fortgang der Reformation Lutheri* (Leipzig, 1717), 1, cited in Fife, p. 588.

not a debate — to determine if he stood by all of his heretical writings or not. And they agreed that if he did stand by those writings they would approve the edict and support the emperor in defense of the religion of their forefathers and the decisions of the councils. On March 6 Charles finally addressed a letter — much to Aleander's chagrin — to "Dear, honored, and pious Dr. Martin Luther," inviting him to appear at Worms within twenty-one days with "information . . . regarding the doctrines and the books which have from time to time come from him," and enclosing a safe-conduct for the journey.[30]

In the meantime the atmosphere at Worms was growing noticeably cold toward the papal representatives, both in the council chambers and on the streets. "Nine-tenths of the people are shouting 'Luther'!" Aleander reported to the papal vice-chancellor, Giulio de Medici (the future Pope Clement VII), "and the other tenth are crying, 'Death to the Roman court'!"[31] At times the nuncio even feared for his own life. And understandably so, since the growing interest in and sympathy for Luther was accompanied by new outbreaks of anticlericalism and antipapalism in many parts of Germany. Some of this antagonism was allayed, especially among the princes, after Aleander delivered a rousing Ash Wednesday speech to the diet, in which he keynoted the position of the prosecution and enlightened the delegates concerning Luther's compromising attitude toward Hus and his derogatory views on the sacraments.[32] So successful, in fact, was Aleander's

30. Fife, p. 628.
31. Fife, p. 619. See Aleander's reports of this antagonism in Paul Kalkoff, ed., *Die Depeschen des Nuntius Aleander vom Wormser Reichstag 1521,* Schriften des Vereins für Reformationsgeschichte, no. 17, especially nos. 5, 6, 7; hereafter cited *Depeschen. See also* Petrus Balan, ed., *Monumenta Reformationis Lutheranae ex Tabulariis secretioribus S. Sedis 1521–1525* (Regensburg: Neo Eboraci & Cincinnatii, 1884), nos. 19, 21, 36; hereafter cited *Monumenta.* Many of these letters are also published in Theodor Brieger, *Aleander und Luther 1521,* Quellen und Forschungen zur Geschichte der Reformation, vol. 1 (Gotha: Friedrich Andreas Perthes, 1884).
32. Reported by Chancellor Brück of Saxony in *Deutsche Reichstagsakten unter Kaiser Karl V,* ed. Adolf Wrede (1896; new edition, Göttingen: Vandenhoeck & Ruprecht, 1962), 2, no. 67; hereafter cited *DRA.* Also see the analysis of this speech in James

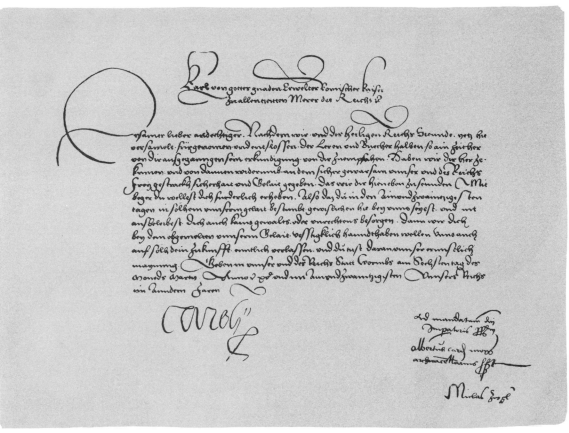

Charles V's summons for Luther to appear at the Diet of Worms, 6 March 1521.

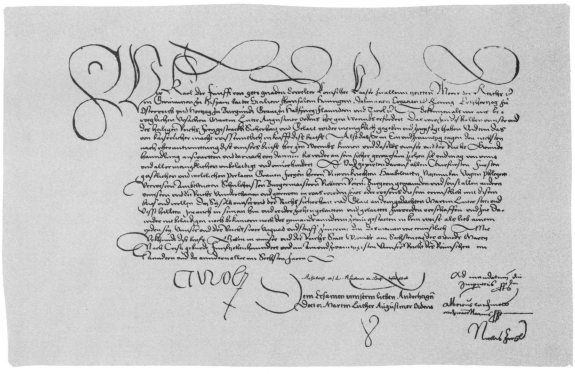

The imperial safe-conduct for Luther to travel to Worms, 6 March 1521.

speech that he gained enough support to have a resolution adopted authorizing him to submit to the diet for its approval the draft of his edict against Luther. Nevertheless, when Luther arrived at the imperial Rhineland city on April 16, after a triumphal two-week progress from Wittenberg, the streets, walls, and rooftops were crowded with cheering followers and curious onlookers. Spalatin had expressed some fear for Luther's life, but Luther assured his friend that even if there were as many devils in Worms as tiles on the roofs, he would still have come. "For," as he later said, "I was unperturbed and unafraid."[33]

At four o'clock the following afternoon, Luther was escorted via back streets — to avoid the boisterous crowds — to the bishop's palace, where the emperor and assembled princes of the empire awaited him. The tension of the moment was extreme. Everyone in the packed hall seemed to sense that Luther's appearance before the diet was the crucial confrontation of the age. The outcome of this encounter would affect all future generations. Every eye was fixed on the now notorious professor. The hum of voices loudened as he entered and took his place near the center of the room facing the emperor and opposite a table stacked with his books. Silence then swept the hall. Soon the secretary to the archbishop of Trier, a close friend and confidant of Aleander, stepped forward to represent the imperial crown. In a strong, clear voice he addressed Luther: "Martin Luther, His Imperial Majesty has summoned you here for these two reasons: first to know whether you publicly acknowledge the authorship of the books there before you bearing your name; and then, whether you stand by them or wish to retract anything in them."[34]

Atkinson, *The Trial of Luther* (London: B. T. Batsford, 1971), pp. 123–31.

33. *Tischreden*, no. 5342b, 5:68–74; Hans J. Hillerbrand, The *Reformation: A Narrative History Related by Contemporary Observers and Participants* (New York: Harper & Row, 1964), p. 93.

34. Although there are several contemporary accounts of the proceedings at Worms, both by Lutheran partisans (Spalatin, Jonas, Luther, etc.) and papal advocates (Aleander, Eck), they are in remarkable agreement on the proceedings and events of the diet. I have used the documents in *DRA*, 2, nos. 79–81, 88; *Monumenta*, no. 68; *WA*, 7:814–87; *LW*, 32:105–31.

Luther at Worms. The upper portion depicts Luther in prayer and below is his entry into the imperial hall. Drawing by Gustav König.

Upon the demand of Luther's lawyer, Dr. Schurff, the titles of the books were then read aloud, and Luther, showing some signs of confusion or trepidation, softly responded,

Two questions have been put to me by His Imperial Majesty: First, whether I wish all the books bearing my name to be regarded as my own work; second, whether I intend to stand by them or, in fact, retract anything from those which have been published by me until now. To these two questions I shall respond briefly and to the point. First, I must indeed include the books just now named as among those written by me, and I shall never deny any of them.

47

Charles V in 1520 just prior to the Diet of Worms. Painting by Bernard van Orley.

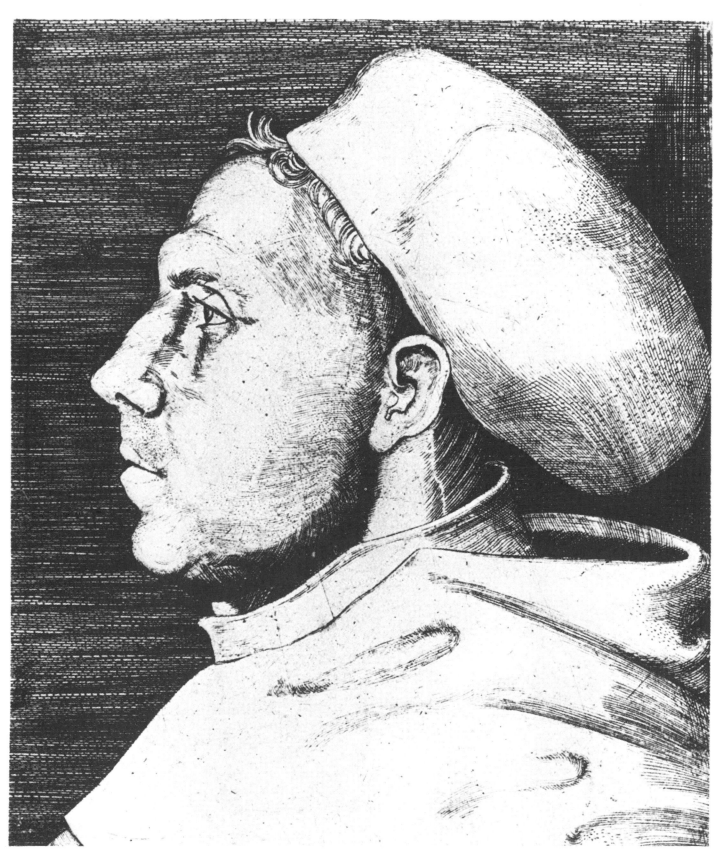

Luther in 1521 at the time of his appearance at Worms. Copper engraving by Lucas Cranach.

As for the next question, whether I would likewise affirm everything or retract what is supposed to have been uttered beyond the testimony of Scripture: Because this is a question of faith and the salvation of souls and because it concerns the divine Word, which we are all bound to reverence, for there is nothing greater in heaven or on earth, it would be rash and at the same time dangerous for me to put forth anything without proper consideration. Since without previous deliberation I could assert less than the cause demands or more than accords with the truth, I might in either case come under Christ's judgment when he said, "Whoever denies me before men, I also will deny before my Father who is in Heaven." For this reason I beseech your Imperial Majesty for time to think, in order to satisfactorily answer the question without violence to the divine Word and danger to my own soul.

The emperor and princes were astonished by this request but after brief consultation agreed to grant Luther twenty-four hours to prepare his reply. Aleander reported to Cardinal de Medici that Luther lost the admiration of many of his followers because of this fainthearted response and hinted that the request for more time might lead to a recantation.

On the following day, April 18, the hearing was moved to a larger hall of the bishop's palace, and because of the pressure of huge crowds outside the building and around every entrance, the session did not resume until nearly six o'clock. The imperial spokesman again put to Luther the question whether he wished to defend all his books or to retract some. This time Luther's reply was firm, even forceful. In a prepared speech he explained that his books were of several kinds.

There are some in which I have discussed religious faith and morals simply and evangelically, so that even my enemies themselves are compelled to admit that these are useful, harmless, and clearly worthy to be read by Christians. . . . Thus, if I should begin to disavow them, I ask you, what would I be doing? Would not I alone of all men be condemning the very truth upon which friends and enemies equally agree . . . ?

Another group of my books attacks the papacy and the papists as those who by their doctrines and their very wicked examples have laid waste the Christian world with evil that affects the spirit and the body. . . . If, therefore, I had retracted these writings, I should have done nothing other than to add strength to this tyranny and I should have

Doctor Martini Luthers offentliche verber zu worms im Reichs tag vor Kai. Ma. Red vnd wider red/am 17·tag Aprilis/im Tausent fünffhundert vnd ainundzwaintzigisten Jar.

Title page of a 1521 pamphlet describing Luther's hearing at Worms. Luther, the emperor, and Aleander are shown.

opened, not only windows, but also doors to such great god-lessness. . . . Good God! What a cover for wickedness and tyranny I should then have become.

At this remark the emperor interrupted to warn Luther to say no more about that subject but to move on to something else. Luther continued:

I have written a third sort of book against some private and (as they say) distinguished individuals [obviously re-ferring to Eck, Emser, Murner, and the like], *namely, those who strive to preserve the Roman tyranny and to destroy the godliness taught by me. Against these I confess I have been more violent than my religion or profession demands. But, then, I do not set myself up as a saint; neither am I disputing about my life, but about the teaching of Christ. It is not proper for me to retract these books, because by this retraction it would again happen that*

51

Luther before Emperor Charles V at Worms. Woodcut from Ludovicus Rabus, *Historien des Heyligen Ausgewählten Gottes Zeugen,* Strasbourg, 1556. Penned in German at the bottom of this picture are the words "Here I stand, I can do nothing else. God help me. Amen."

tyranny and godlessness would, with my patronage, rule and rage among the people of God more violently than ever before.

For another ten minutes or more Luther continued to expound the reason and justification for his writings, to confess his discipleship of Christ, and to call upon the members of the assembly to instruct him if he erred. At that the secretary reprimanded him for his impertinence, declaring that he was mistaken to set himself up as the sole authority on doctrine, against the combined wisdom of the church, and that he was simply repeating the errors of the Waldenses, of Wyclif, and of Hus before him, and demanded once and for all a simple, direct, and unambiguous answer to the question. Would he revoke his books and errors?

Luther's final reply was brief and bold:

Since, then, Your Serene Majesty and Your Lordships ask for a simple answer, I will give it in this manner without horns or teeth: Unless I am convinced by the testimony of Scripture or by clear reason (for I trust neither pope nor councils alone, since it is well known that they have often erred and contradicted themselves), I am bound by the Scriptures I have cited, for my conscience is captive to the word of God. I cannot and will not retract anything, since

Doctor Martini Luthers offen-
liche Verhör zů Worms im Reichs tag/
Red/ Vnd Widerred Am. 17. tag/
Aprilis/ Jm jar 1521
Beschechen

Copia ainer Missiue/ Doctor Martinus Luther nach seinem abschid zů Worms zů rugck an die Churfür
sten/ Fürsten/ Vñ stend des Reichs da selbst
verschriben gesamlet hatt.

Luther before the emperor and Diet of Worms. Title page from Spalatin's pamphlet, *Martin Luther's public Hearing at Worms before the Reichstag* (Augsburg, 1521), containing Luther's account of the proceedings.

Luther's confrontation with the emperor at the Diet of Worms. Nineteenth-century painting by Anton von Werner.

Philipp Melanchthon

to act against one's conscience is neither safe nor right. God help me, Amen![35]

A few more verbal volleys were exchanged before the prosecutor admonished Luther: "Lay aside your conscience, Martin. You must lay it aside, because it is in error; and it will be safe and proper for you to recant. Although you say the councils have erred, you will never be able to prove it, in matters of faith at least; and even in matters of morals I fancy it will be with much difficulty." As the meeting adjourned, Luther shouted back that he was able and willing to do that too.

But the drama was not yet over. The emperor was still to be heard. He had listened intently and silently to Luther's speech. What would be his reaction to Luther's stand? If he desired unity and support from the German princes (and he certainly did), it might logically have entered his mind that the wisest move would be to throw in his lot with the reformer. It was obvious that Luther had many friends, even among the princes and electors, and that the German temperament was violently antagonistic toward Rome. If Charles should openly defy the pope (who certainly did not always support Charles) and renounce papal authority in the empire — as Henry VIII would do in England just ten years later — he might become the leader of a unified German nation. Later pundits, including Napoleon I, have accused the emperor of shortsightedness for his failure to seize the moment. But in so reasoning they have totally ignored the reality of religious conviction in Charles's thought and behavior. That there was ever a chance for the success of such a scheme — even if the emperor had entertained it — is questionable in the first place. And it is highly improbable that it ever entered his mind. Charles's short but pointed reply to Luther, written in French in his own hand and read in German the following day to the assembled estates, testifies to his undeviating loyalty

35. The colorful "Here I Stand" flourish seems to have been added to the printed text of the speech as an afterthought. In the Latin version of the Worms encounter this phrase is inserted in German: "Ich kan nicht anders, hie stehe ich, Got helff mir, Amen." *WA,* 7:838; *DRA,* 2:555; *LW,* 32:113.

to the church and to the unity of Christendom:

You know that I am descended from the most Christian emperors of the noble German nation, from the Catholic Kings of Spain, the archdukes of Austria, and the dukes of Burgundy, who were all to the death true sons of the Roman church, defenders of the Catholic faith and of its sacred customs, decrees, rituals and ordinances. They have bequeathed all this to me as my heritage, to live and die according to their example, which I have hitherto done. For this reason I am determined to hold fast to all that has happened since the Council of Constance. For it is certain that a single monk must err in his opinion if he stands against all of Christendom; otherwise, Christendom itself would have erred for more than a thousand years.

Therefore, I am determined to set my kingdoms and dominions, my friends, my body, my blood, my life, and my soul upon it. For it would be a great shame to me and to you, who are the noble and renowned German nation, called to be defenders and protectors of the Catholic faith, if in our time through our negligence we were to let heresy, or even the appearance of heresy, and the repudiation of true religion enter the hearts of men. After having heard the obstinate answer which Luther gave yesterday in the presence of us all, I declare to you that I regret having so long delayed to proceed against him. I shall not hear him again. I order that he return [to Wittenberg] according to his safe-conduct, but that he no longer preach nor admonish the people with his falsehoods. Henceforth, I shall proceed against him as a notorious heretic, and I request that you all conduct yourselves in this matter as good Christians, as you have promised to do.[36]

Thus the gauntlet was thrown down — and accepted. What followed seemed anticlimactic. That is why it is usually overlooked by historians. But there were still two important acts before the spectacle would be finished. Following the emperor's declaration and the drawing up of a procedural paper by Elector Joachim of Brandenburg, the electoral council voted to carry out the imperial ban.[37] But angry threats from Luther's supporters in and around Worms, pressure from Frederick of Saxony to allow Luther a scholarly hearing, and the pricking consciences of those members of the diet who knew they had not given the Wittenberger the oppor-

---

36. *DRA*, 2:595–96.
37. *Monumenta*, no. 69.

Vous sauez que ie suis descendu des empereurs tres chrestiens de la noble natio
mainque des roys catholiques despaigne, des archeducs daustrie des Ducz de
Bourgoingne, les quelz tous ont estez iusques a la mort filz fideles de leglise
Romaine ayant tousiours este deffenseurs de la foy sacrspligue des sacrees
cerimonies decretz ordonnances et sainctes coustumes a lhonneur de dieu augmenta
cion de la foy et salut des ames, Apres leur trespas des quelz par droit na
turel et heritaige nous ont laysez les dictes sainctes obseruations catholiques
pour y vivre et mourir a leur exemple es quelle comme vray imitateur
diceulx noz predecesseurs auons par la grace de dieu iusques a ycy vescu
A ceste cause ie suis delibere denteteni tout ce que mes dictz predecesseurs
et moy auons entretenu iusques au present Et par especial ce que de sie
ordonne par les dictz mes predecesseurs tant au concile de constence que autres
Car yl est certain que ung seul frere erre en son opinion la quelle est
contre tout la crestiennete tant du temps passe mille ans et plus que au
present selon la quelle opinion toute la dicte crestiennite seroit et auroit
tousiours este en erreur, par quoy suis determine toutellement y employ
yer mes royaulmes et seigneuries, mes amis, mon corps, mon sanc, ma vie
et mon ame, Car ce seroit grant honte amoy et a vous que estes la noble
et renommee nation de germanie qui sommes par priuilege et preemi
nence singuliers iustitues deffenseurs et protecteurs de la foy sacrspligue
que en nre temps non seullement heresie mes suspicion de heresie ou dimmu
tion de la religion crestienne par nre negligence demeure apres nous et au
taiges des hommes aure perpetuel deshonneur et de noz successeurs, Et ouyt
la responce pertinace que Luthere donna hier en la presence de nous tous
Je vous declaire que me repens dauoir tant du lavc aproceder contre led
Luthere et sa faulse doctrine Et ne suis delibere depuis oultre loyr yler
mais Je entens que incontinant selon la forme du mandat quel soit re
mene sen gardant la teneur de son sauf conduyt sans prescher ny ad
monester le peuple de sa manluaise doctrine et sans procurer que
aulcune esmotion esface Et comme cy dessus ay dit suis delibere me
conduyre et proceder a lencontre de luy comme contre notoire eretique
vous requerant que vous voz declairez en ceste affaire comme bons chrestiens
et estes tenuz le faire et le mauez promis, fait de ma main ce xix da
brie de 1521, Signe, Carolus

Collacionne au vray original
escript de la main de lempereur

Lalemand

Copy of Charles V's reply to Luther, 19 April 1521. Written by the emperor in French.

Luther at the Diet of Worms. Relief from the Luther Monument in Worms.

tunity to argue his case nor even hear the Catholic case expounded, moved the diet to try another tack, against Aleander's opposition.[38] Taking Luther at his word that he would accept scriptural proof of his errors, the diet appointed a commission of learned men to reason with Luther. The commission included such illustrious persons as the archbishop of Trier, the bishop of Brandenburg, the bishop of Augsburg, Elector Joachim of Brandenburg, Duke George of Saxony, Dietrich von Cleen (master of the Teutonic Knights), Count George of Wertheim, Dr. Hans Bock of Strasbourg, Dr. Peutinger of Augsburg, and Dr. Vehus of Baden. For two days these princes and professors made a genuine attempt to find a formula for reconciliation with Luther. But they had few concessions to offer him, and Luther was unwilling to budge from his own doctrinal positions unless *he* were convinced by

38. *Depeschen,* no. 21, especially pp. 146–49, Aleander to Giulio de Medici; *Monumenta,* no. 74. The diet's communication to the emperor is printed in *Monumenta,* no. 71; *DRA,* 2, no. 84.

Statue of Martin Luther by Ernst Rietschel, comprising the central portion of the Luther Monument in Worms.

scripture that he was wrong. Nothing that any of the commissioners could say moved him in the least.[39]

Following this failure, Luther was summoned to several private interviews, first with the archbishop of Trier and his secretary, and then with Johann Cochlaeus, a former follower of Luther who had changed sides at Worms and had become an outspoken opponent. Luther's stubborn stand is represented in his answer to the archbishop: "I would rather lose my life and head than desert the crystal-clear Word of God."[40] With this unbending confidence that his interpretation of scripture was in fact the word of God, there remained little room for compromise. As far as Luther was concerned, the matter was out of his hands: there were no grounds for negotiation; he followed only when the word led him. A year later Luther wrote,

Johann Cochlaeus

I simply taught, preached, and wrote God's Word; otherwise, I did nothing. And then, while I slept or drank Wittenberg beer with my Philip and my Amsdorf, the Word so greatly weakened the Papacy that never a Prince or Emperor inflicted such damage upon it. I did nothing. The Word did it all. Had I desired to foment trouble, I could have brought great bloodshed upon Germany. Yea, I could have started such a little game at Worms that the Emperor would not have been safe. But what would it have been? A mug's game. I left it to the Word.[41]

---

39. *DRA,* 2, nos. 85–87, pp. 599–632. *See also* Atkinson, *The Trial of Luther,* pp. 164–78.

40. Atkinson, *The Trial of Luther,* p. 174.

41. *Works of Martin Luther.* trans. C. M. Jacobs et al., 6 vols. (Philadelphia: A. J. Holman Co., 1915–32), 2:399. *See also* Rupp, p. 99.

The Edict of Worms

n spite of the decisiveness of Luther's stand at Worms, the members of the diet were hesitant to publish a formal ban against him even though they had previously agreed to support the emperor. And Charles could not legally issue the edict without the concurrence of the assembled estates. Some of the electors were sympathetic to Luther's cause, particularly Frederick of Saxony and the Count Palatine; others were reluctant to take too strong a stand against him for fear of political repercussions. Franz von Sickingen had already threatened to descend on Worms with an army if Luther were harmed. "We have Franz on our side," wrote Ulrich von Hutten on May 1, "and he is not merely favorably disposed, but is red hot and burning."[42] Four hundred other nobles were rumored to have pledged their arms in his support. Francesco Cornaro, the Venetian ambassador at Worms, reported in January that Luther had 40,000 followers, although Cornaro's secretary, Andrea Rosso, judged that it was more like 20,000.[43] Following Luther's last appearance before the diet, placards bearing the frightening emblem of the *Bundschuh,* symbol of the peasant leagues, were found posted on doors near the imperial residence. Some of these demonstrations singled out the papal nuncio for particularly scurrilous attack. One Spanish account of the events at Worms tells of obscene pictures labelled "Hieronymus" and coarse, abusive signs attacking him.[44]

It was not primarily fear, however, that prevented the delegates at Worms from immediately supporting the emperor's wish to publish an edict against the

42. Johannes Janssen, *History of the German People at the Close of the Middle Ages,* trans. A. M. Christie, 3rd ed. rev., 17 vols. (New York: AMS Press, 1966), 3:197–98.

43. Marino Sanuto, *Diarii,* 29:572–73, 617–19, quoted in Paul Kalkoff, ed., *Briefe, Depeschen und Berichte über Luther vom Wormser Reichstag 1521,* Schriften des Vereins für Reformationsgeschichte, no. 59, pp. 26, 31.

44. "Despues desto parecieron por ciertas partes de la ciudad de Bormes unas figuras pintadas en papel negras y disformes, y decia la letra Gerónimo; . . . Tambien estaban escritas ciertas copias en Aleman en injuria del dicho Gerónimo, nuncio del papa." *DRA,* 2:637. *See also* p. 559; *Depeschen,* no. 21, pp. 146–47.

Franz von Sickingen

Title page of a 1513 pamphlet depicting the activities of the
Bundschuh. The peasants on the right are shown swearing al-
legiance to the league.

heretical writings of Martin Luther. They were
jealous of their constitutional right to discuss and
help formulate any decree issued in behalf of the
diet. Normally a commission should have been appointed to draft the edict. Such a commission had in
fact been created for this purpose in January, under
the chairmanship of the archbishop of Salzburg, but
the archbishop had since quarreled with the imperial court and had gone home in a huff. Therefore,
hoping for speedier action in the face of impending
war with France, Charles, instead of turning to a
new committee, appointed Aleander to draft a document.[45]

---

45. Paul Kalkoff, *Die Entstehung des Wormser Edikts* (Leipzig:
Verlag von M. Heinsius Nachfolger, 1913), pp. 195–97. Cf. Johannes
Kühn, "Zur Entstehung des Wormser Edikt," *Zeitschrift für
Kirchengeschichte,* 35 (1914):372–92, 529–47.

On May 1, less than twenty-four hours after he had received the nod to prepare the edict, Aleander presented a Latin draft to Chancellor Gattinara who immediately turned it over to the Imperial Court Council (*Reichshofrat*). The council was not pleased with the draft, disliking its style and some of its content. Discusssion and revision followed, after which a German translation was made by two of the imperial secretaries. Chancellor Gattinara, Aleander's liaison with the council and with the emperor, promised the impatient members that versions would also be provided in French and Flemish.[46] The German version was put into chancellery form, changing the tone somewhat and deleting unacceptable passages, such as the inferences that the imperial authority was subordinate to the papal and that a notorious heretic like Luther should not be heard by lay princes. These notions were completely suppressed in the German translation.[47] Other revisions and deletions were made, and on May 8 the edict was accepted by the council and made ready for the emperor's signature.

The document reemphasized the danger of heresies and false doctrines leading the faithful followers of Christ into error and the nations into schism. It recounted the steps taken by the papacy and by the emperor to bring Martin Luther back to repentance and obedience. His many errors were enumerated, from disturbing and condemning the sacraments to attacking the authority of the general councils and the pope. Such a rebellious and evil man, continued the edict, was not worthy to be considered or treated as a Christian. The events of Worms were reviewed and the conclusion reached that Luther was an "obstinate, schismatic heretic," who should be apprehended and duly punished. Furthermore, his accomplices and anyone who aided him in any way were also under imperial condemnation — an obvious allusion to Elector Frederick of Saxony, who even then was giving asylum to Luther at Wartburg. His books were not to be bought, sold, kept, or read by anyone; and all existing copies were

---

46. Kalkoff, *Die Entstehung*, p. 237.
47. *DRA*, 2:649, 655. Paquier, p. 271.

to be burned. And the writings and drawings of others who sympathized with and supported Luther should be treated in the same manner. Printers or booksellers were ordered to have nothing to do with such heretical materials, to the extent that printers had to obtain permission before they were authorized even to mention the scriptures or their interpretation. This document was presented to Charles V on May 12.

But the emperor, cautious in the face of renewed demonstrations by Lutheran supporters following the news of Luther's abduction near Eisenach, and not wanting to alienate the princes by taking action without full approval of the diet, hesitated to sign the edict. Until he had secured the formal cooperation of the German estates in the war against France, he was loath to sign a document that they had not fully approved and that would outlaw many of Charles's subjects along with Luther.

Aleander was distraught. The imperial edict he had worked so long to obtain, and which now more than ever was imperative, seemed to be slipping away. His concern was compounded by the continuing difficulty of obtaining a satisfactory papal bull against Luther. Although the bull of excommunication, *Decet Romanum,* was dated 3 January 1521, it was not immediately published and would not technically be in effect until such a formal presentation took place. It was Aleander's job to accomplish this. By February 12 he had received a copy of the bull but found it to contain so many errors "inimical to our cause" (especially the inclusion of the names of Ulrich von Hutten, Wilibald Pirkheimer, Lazare Spengler, and others along with Luther's) that he was afraid to have it published in that form. Two weeks before Luther's appearance at Worms, Aleander wrote to Rome requesting a new bull to replace *Decet Romanum.* In it, he emphasized,

There is no need to mention Hutten or anyone except Luther, because there are people here who argue that they do not know whether Luther was actually declared a heretic or not at the end of the grace period, and they use this excuse to favor him. Besides, it is not a good time to publish the former bull because Hutten and all these nobles will murder me even though I am close to the emperor.... I still intend to publish this bull mentioning Hutten, but after I am safely out of Germany. God forbid that it be published while we are at Worms, for it will do our cause no good, and will cost us our lives.[48]

Ulrich von Hutten

As late as April 29 the new bull still had not arrived, and Aleander pleaded with the pope to hurry. "Give it the same date as the previous one, January 3, and for the love of God, do it quickly!"[49] Finally, on May 8, just as the German council was redrafting the Edict of Worms, the nuncio reported that the bull had been received. Aleander responded to the papal vice-chancellor,

After I had written and sealed my other letter, your letter and the bull (wherein only Luther is mentioned by name, his supporters being referred to in general terms) arrived. It came at the right moment, but I wish it had been sent somewhat sooner, for I would have published it here . . . and we would have mentioned it in the edict, which is now in advanced stage and cannot be delayed. Furthermore, since some evil is stirring here [sì perchè subito nasce qualche mal] and since the emperor is threatening to leave soon, I doubt that we have much time.[50]

But now some of the council, including the archbishop of Mainz, objected to the bull, and it was not until after the publication of the Edict of Worms that the bull of excommunication finally was published.

Two more weeks passed before any further action was taken on the edict by the emperor, even though Aleander continued to plead for action. In the meantime the diet was reduced in numbers to a mere skeleton, many of its members having fled Worms to escape the plague that had broken out there toward the end of April. The archbishop of Mainz, the elector Palatine of the Rhine, and the elector of Saxony had all left, as had many other princes, prelates, and

---

48. *Monumenta,* no. 61, p. 158; Brieger, pp. 129–30; *Depeschen,* no. 16, pp. 113–22. The controversy over the bull is clearly summarized by Roland H. Bainton in "Problems in Luther Biography," *Studies on the Reformation* (Boston: Beacon Press, 1966), pp. 93–96.

49. *Monumenta,* no. 94, p. 240, incorrectly dated May 23; Brieger, p. 169.

50. *Monumenta,* no. 89, p. 224, incorrectly dated May 15; Brieger, pp. 191–92. *See also* Kalkoff, *Die Entstehung,* p. 242.

Emperor Charles V ten years after the Diet of Worms. Contemporary engraving.

burghers. On May 23 the remaining princes agreed to support the emperor's war effort and his projected pilgrimage to Rome to receive the papal coronation. Charles in turn reached an understanding with Pope Leo whereby the papacy would also assist the emperor against France in return for his promise to proceed hastily against the Lutheran heresy.[51]

On May 25 the diet met in its last formal session. Two papal briefs addressed to the emperor and to the German princes, respectively, complimenting them on their good judgment in handling the Luther affair, were read. At the same time they were exhorted to persevere until this new heresy was completely rooted out.[52] At three o'clock in the afternoon the solemn ceremony of cloture took place, and the Diet of Worms was officially ended. However, in his closing speech Charles asked as many of the delegates as could to stay an additional four days to conclude the final work of the diet.[53] To this rump session, composed of three electors (the archbishops of Cologne and Trier, and Margrave Joachim of Brandenburg) and a few other princes and bishops, Charles presented the council-approved edict. It is obvious that the emperor had been influenced by Aleander's persistent arguments and by his own fears that it would be unwise to risk presenting the edict to the entire diet. By this ruse the edict would have the appearance of Reichstag approval without the danger of being drastically watered down or disapproved. Although still somewhat dissatisfied with the violence of the Aleandrean language, these delegates, mostly conservative Catholics, approved the Edict of Worms as it was presented to them — without changing "a single jot," according to the elector of Brandenburg.

The next day, May 26, exactly one month after Luther had departed from the imperial city, Charles V signed the original parchment Latin and German versions of the edict, both dated May 8, thereby strengthening the impression that it had the approval of the whole diet. After the signing, a solemn public

---

51. Kalkoff, *Die Entstehung*, p. 236.
52. *Monumenta,* nos. 84, 86, pp. 218–22; Paquier, pp. 263–64.
53. Paquier, p. 262.

proclamation, or mandate of publication, was read and subsequently circulated to all parts of the empire. This imperial letter announced the publication of the Edict of Worms, drawn up "by the consent and will" of the diet (*mit rat und willen unser und des heiligen reiches churfürsten, fürsten und stende*), and called upon all authorities in the empire and in Charles's inherited territories to treat this edict with "utmost gravity," to study it carefully, and to have it publicly proclaimed in their lands, or they themselves would be subject to the penalties enumerated in the document.[54]

Publication of the Edict of Worms began immediately. Even before the emperor had affixed his signature to the document, Aleander had advanced a deposit of ten gold florins to the Worms printer Hans von Erfurt to prepare the German version for publication. This printed edition (completed between May 26 and 30), rather than the manuscript original signed by the emperor, became the official text for the empire.[55] It was considerably altered from Aleander's Latin manuscript, having undergone modifications in the council that made the text less offensive to Germans.

Aleander left Worms on May 31 in the suite of the emperor. Parting with the imperial train at Cologne on June 11, the nuncio proceeded to Louvain, where, between June 19 and 26, he had the first Latin edition of the edict published by Theodore Martinus.[56] Aleander translated this version into French himself and had it published at Antwerp[57] along with a Flemish translation commissioned by him.[58]

---

54. *DRA*, 2, no. 93, pp. 659–61.

55. Ziegler and Spiegel's Latin translation ("Acta Wormacensia," fols. 141–54) and the original German manuscript are found in the Vatican Archives. The German printed text is located in *DRA*, 2:640–59.

56. Nijhoff-Kronenberg, *Nederlandsche Bibliographie van 1500 tot 1540*, 3 vols. in 6 (The Hague: Martinus Nijhoff, 1940), 2, no. 3298, p. 523. "Acta Wormacensia," fols. 130–38. The original Latin manuscript is located in the Vatican Archives under Arm. 2, cap. 1, no. 92.

57. Nijhoff-Kronenberg, 2, no. 3303, p. 526. Published by Claes de Grave? "Acta Wormacensia," fols. 157–65.

58. Nijhoff-Kronenberg, 2, no. 3299, p. 524. Published by Claes de Grave? "Acta Wormacensia," fols. 167–75. *See also* Paquier, pp. viii–ix, 271–72.

The copy of the Edict of Worms acquired by the J. Reuben Clark, Jr., Library at Brigham Young University is one of the very few contemporary texts of the edict still in existence and is perhaps the only copy of this edition. It is a French version published in Paris, apparently by the printer Pierre Gromors. It is taken directly from Aleander's Antwerp edition with few variations. The format and arrangement of charges against Luther are somewhat altered from the printed German text, adhering closely to the Latin. But the content is essentially the same. Strongly worded, sweeping, and repetitive, the document is a superb example — along with Luther's equally strong declarations at Worms — of the dogmatic inflexibility of the religious upheaval of the sixteenth century. It is easy to see why many of the princes were reluctant to have it published and why those who supported it found enforcing it to be impossible.

The Reformation spread rapidly throughout western and northern Europe in the next few decades in spite of the Edict of Worms. Protestant adherents came from every walk of life and from every country, each with his own motives and justifications. Some joined for social and economic reasons, some for political and dynastic advantage. Many left the Catholic Church because of its ecclesiastical and moral abuses, others because they found more spiritual and devotional satisfaction in the Lutheran worship (or in subsequent Zwinglian, Calvinist, or Anabaptist devotions). A few became Protestants because they were converted to Luther's way of interpreting scripture and his belief in the independent saving grace of God.

For the Catholic Church the Edict of Worms was a political document authorizing the apprehension and punishment of Lutheran heretics. But more than that, it was a succinct statement of grievances against Luther and an unequivocal condemnation of his doctrines. After the confrontation at Worms, Catholics needed only to refer to the "Edict" to justify their persecution of anyone with undesirable or unpopular ideas. It became the symbol of the budding Counter-Reformation.

Text of
the Edict of
Worms [59]

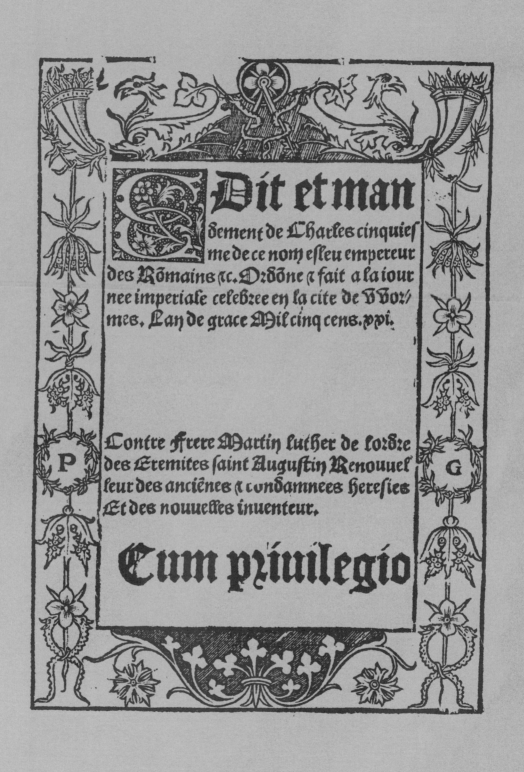

Dit et man
dement de Charles cinquies
me de ce nom esleu empereur
des Rômains ꝛc. Ordône ꝛ fait a la iour
nee imperiale celebree en la cite de Wor̄/
mes. Lan de grace Mil cinq cens. xxi.

Contre frere Martin luther de lordre
des Eremites saint Augustin Renouuel
leur des anciênes ꝛ condamnees heresies
Et des nouuelles inuenteur.

Cum priuilegio

dict and mandate of Charles, Fifth of this name, Emperor Elect of the Romans,[60] ordered and written on the imperial day celebrated in the city of Worms. In the year of our Lord one thousand five hundred twenty-one.

Against brother Martin Luther of the order of the Saint Augustinian Eremites, reviver of the old and condemned heresies and inventor of new ones.

By permission.[61]

---

59. Translated by De Lamar Jensen and Jacquelin Delbrouwire.

60. Charles was elected German emperor in the imperial city of Frankfurt on 28 June 1519 by the electoral college (established by the Golden Bull of 1356), made up of the king of Bohemia, the margrave of Brandenburg, the elector of Saxony, the count Palatine of the Rhine, and the archbishops of Mainz, Trier, and Cologne. He was subsequently crowned at Aachen on 23 October 1520. Technically, his title was only King of the Romans, or Emperor Elect, until his subsequent coronation by the pope, symbolizing the combined secular-religious partnership of the Holy Roman Empire. For Charles this last event did not take place until 24 February 1530, after the imperial sack of Rome had forced Clement VII to concede to many of the emperor's demands. This was the last time the emperors ever bothered with the papal coronation.

61. This title page is adorned with a handsome woodcut border bearing the initials of the printer, probably Pierre Gromors. The edict is bound by Godillot in modern red morocco with gilt edges and gilt dentelles.

¶Contre tous et chascuns liures et escriptures soubz le nom dudit Luther desia publiez ou a publier. Et aussi contre ceulx qui doresenauant imprimeront/acheteront ou Venderõt iceulx liures ou escriptures.

¶Item Contre les complices recepuans ᶜ en quelque manie re que ce soit fauorisans audit Luther ᶜ ses oeuures.

¶Item Contre tous ᶜ chascuns liures diffamatoires ᶜ iniur rieux. Et aussi aultres semblables escriptures ᶜ peinctures. Et diceulx ou icelles aucteurs imprimeurs/achepteurs ou Vẽ deurs de quelque nom. degre ou condition quilz soyent.

¶Loy pour les imprimeurs pour deffẽdre les maulx qui pro uiẽnent par le mauuais abus du louable artifice de limpressiõ.

¶Les peines.

¶De crime de lese Maieste ᶜ tresgriefue offense ᶜ indignation du prince ᶜc.

¶Item Confiscacion ᶜ perte de corps ᶜ tous ᶜ chascuns biẽs meubles ᶜ immeubles. Desquelz la moitie appartiendra au sei gneur. Et lautre moitie aux accusateurs ou denonciateurs. Auec les aultres peines comprinses es droitz. Comme appert plus amplement en ce present edit ᶜ mandement.

Against each and every one of the books and writings under the name of the said Luther already published or to be published, and also against those who henceforth will print, buy, or sell those books and writings.[62]

Item. Against accomplices receiving or favoring Luther and his works in any way.

Item. Against all insulting and libelous books, and other such writings and illustrations, and also against writers, printers, buyers, or sellers, whoever they are or whatever social status or condition they have.

Law for printers to defend against the evils which come from the abuse of the praiseworthy craft of printing.

Punishments

For the crime of *lèse majesté* [high treason][63] and for very serious offense and indignation against the prince.

Item. Confiscation and loss of body and belongings and all goods, fixed and movable, half of which will go to the Lord, and the other half to the accusers and denouncers. With other punishments as given more fully in the present edict and mandate.

---

62. This first inside page is a resumé of the main contents of the edict, summarizing the principal charges against Luther and the penalties enacted against him and his supporters.

63. *Lèse majesté* is an offense, affront, or crime committed against the dignity and/or authority of the sovereign. In the sixteenth century it was a most serious crime.

Harles par la divi-

ne clemence esleu empereur des Rommains/roy
de Castille ꞇ Archiduc daustrice ꞇc. A noz gou-
uerneurs des royaulmes/ terres/ seigneuries et
gens de conseil de nostre empire. Et aussi a tous ꞇ quelcõques
noz subgectz de nosditz pays de quelque estat/dignite/ou condi
tion quilz soient/ausquelz cestuy nostre present edit/decret/ꞇ oz
donnance sera monstre/ Salut ꞇ grace. ꞆA lhõneur et louenge
de dieu nostre createur/par la clemence duquel nous a este don
ne les royaumes/terres ꞇ seigneuries dessusdictes/nous appar
tient ayder a subiuguer les ennemys de nostre foy a lobedience
de sa diuine maieste/Ampliant la gloire de la croix et passion
de nostre seigneur(autant que en nous sera). Et de tenir necte ꞇ
pure la religion crestiẽne de toute peste dheresie/ou suspition di
celle/selon ꞇ ensuyuant lordonnance ꞇ coustume par cy deuant
obseruee en la saincte eglise Rõmaine. A quoy sommes enclin
singulierement par cueur ferme et fidele/tant de nous mesmes
cõme de noz predecesseurs et geniteurs/ lesquelz par la grace de
dieu ont persecute les ennemys de nostre foy/ bannys hors de
leurs possessions ꞇ seigneuries/ꞇ par labeurs/despens/perilz in-
dicibles augmẽte ꞇ preserue la possession de la foy de nostre saul
ueur Jesucrist/incessamment prenans a cueur que nulle appa-
rance ou ligiere suspition de heresie ou infidelite apparoissent
en leursditz royaulmes ꞇ seigneuries. Pour ceste cause apres a
uoir certainement cõgneu les erreurs ꞇ heresies que vng quidã
nõme Martin luther de lordre des Eremites saint Augustin/
A contre nostre foy catholique ꞇ la saincte Rõmaine ꞇ vniuer
sele eglise enseigne iniquement/presche faulcement/ꞇescript tant
en latin que en Alemand detestablement/ ce qui est desia diuulgue quasi partoute crestiente/ mesmement en aucunes de noz
terres ꞇ seigneuries/a la grant diminution de lhõneur de dieu et
de la foy catholique/peril ꞇ dangier des ames crestiẽnes/ ꞇ con-

A.ii.

Charles, by divine grace emperor of the Romans, king of Castile, and archduke of Austria, to our governors of kingdoms, lands, domains, and members of the council of our empire and to all the subjects of our lands, from whatever state, dignity, or condition they may be, and to which our present edict, decree, and ordinance will be shown, greetings.

To the honor and praise of God, our creator, through whose mercy we have been given kingdoms, lands, and domains hereabove mentioned, it is our duty to help subdue the enemies of our faith and bring them to the obedience of the divine majesty, magnifying the glory of the cross and the passion of our Lord (insofar as we are able), and to keep the Christian religion pure from all heresy or suspicion of heresy, according to and following the ordinance and custom observed by the Holy Roman Church. We are rooted in that faith with a true heart, like our predecessors and progenitors, who by the grace of God also persecuted the enemies of our faith and banished them from their lands.[64] Through their labors, expenditures, and indescribable perils, they have augmented and preserved the faith of our Savior Jesus Christ. They were unceasingly concerned that no appearance or suspicion of heresy or unfaithfulness appear in their kingdoms and domains. For this reason — after having learned of the mistakes and heresies of a certain Martin Luther, of the order of the Eremites of Saint Augustine, who teaches iniquity, preaches false doctrines, and writes, in both Latin and German, evil things against our Catholic faith and the Holy Roman and Universal Church, things which have already been spread throughout almost all of Christendom, and abusively into some of our lands and domains, greatly diminishing the honor of God and the Catholic faith, imperiling and endangering Christian souls,

---

64. The church and the empire had frequently cooperated in the extirpation of heresy in the later middle ages: Emperor Frederick I (Barbarossa), for example, supported the branding of the Waldenses as heretics in 1184. More celebrated are Emperor Sigismund's "crusades" against the Hussites in Germany and Bohemia (1415–36).

fusion pour le temps aduenir de toute la chose publicque de no
stre mere saincte eglise/tellement que si ordre ny estoit briefue/
ment donnee telle confusion contagieuse pourroit estre a la cor/
ruption de toutes fideles nations / au peril de tomber en abo/
minables scismes ¬ detestable sentement de nostre saincte foy.
¶Et aussi apres auoir este aduertis q̃ pour icelles choses no/
stre saint pere le pape Leon diziesme de ce nom comme pasteur
general de leglise vniuersele auquel appartient principalement
mettre ordre aux choses qui concernent nostre saincte foy et les
sacremens de leglise/feist admonnester doulcement ¬ charitable
ment ledit Martin luther de soy deporter desditz erreurs ¬ faul
ses doctrines/¬de iceulx legitimemẽt(cõme a tel cas appartiẽt)
reuocquer ¬ soy desdire/ce que si dit Martin non seulemẽt ref/
fusa de faire/Mais(que pis est) adiousta nouueaulx erreurs
pires et plus abominables que les vremiers/lesquelz sema par
tous pays ¬ cõtrees ou luy fut possible. Parquoy icelluy nostre
saint pere le Pape fut diligent de vser des remẽdes accoustu/
mez ¬ opportuns pour obuier a telles pestilences/ et souuentes/
foys conuocant les tresreuerendz cardinaulx de la saincte egli
se rommaine. Jointz plusieurs aultres prelatz ecclesiastiques/
Cestassauoir archeuesques/eues q̃s/ les generaulx des ordres
mendians/¬ prelatz de diuerses regions/ensemble plusieurs no
tables docteurs tant en theologie cõme droit canon et ciuil/ et
aultres facultez de bõne renõmee/conscience/¬ sciẽce excellente/
tant en sens cõme en congnoissance de diuerses langues/apres
auoir cite canoniquement ¬ iuridiquement ledit Martin luther
luy offrant toute asseurance/¬ attendu longuement sil reuien/
droit a cõgnoissance/¬ voyant finablemẽt que ledit Leuther de
mouroit obstine ¬ contumax/nostredict saint pere du conseil et
cõsentement des dessusditz cardinaulx/¬ par aduis ¬ meure deli
beration desditz prelatz et docteurs/ par auctorite apostolique
condamna ¬ reprouua les liures dudit Luther/les iugeant per
nicieux ¬ contraires a nostre foy/lunion ¬ charite de nostre me

and bringing future confusion to all the public affairs of our Holy Mother Church — if we do not put an end to this contagious confusion, it could lead to the corrupting of all faithful nations and to their falling into abominable schisms.

Furthermore, after having been informed of these things, our Holy Father, Pope Leo X, general pastor of the Universal Church (to whom belongs the right to bring order into all matters pertaining to our faith and to the church sacraments), kindly admonished the said Martin Luther to rid himself of these errors and false doctrines, and, as is appropriate, asked him to renounce these doctrines definitively. Martin not only refused to do this but, what is even worse, added new errors even more despicable and abominable than the first and spread his doctrines over all the country (wherever he could). Our Holy Father was diligent to find cures for such pestilences and very often has assembled the cardinals of the Holy Roman Church, as well as several other ecclesiastical prelates (i.e., archbishops, bishops, generals of various orders, and prelates of different areas), several well-known doctors of theology and of canon and civil law, and other men renowned for their common sense, their learning, and their knowledge of languages. After canonically and juridically citing Martin Luther, offering him every assurance and expecting him to come back to a better judgment, but seeing that Luther remained obstinate, our Holy Father, with the cardinals' consent, after deliberation by the prelates and doctors and by the apostolic authority which he holds, condemned the said Luther's books and judged them to be pernicious and against our faith and the union and charity of our Holy Mother Church.

Emperor Maximilian I

re saincte eglise/Decernant que lesditz liures en quelques langues quilz fussent escriptz fussent bruslez τ ostez perpetuellemēt
de la memoire des hōmes. ¶Et quant a icelluy Martin sil ne
se recōgnoissoit τ retournoit a penitence/cōgnoissant τ reuocant
sa faulte et sesditz erreurs dedans certain temps lors a luy assi-
gne/le declaira inobediant τ enfant diniquite/scismatique τ he-
retique/τ cōme tel deuoit estre deboute/τ selon lordōnance τ disposition des droitz puny soubz les censures contenues es bulles apostoliques surce depeschees. Lesquelles par honnorable
hōme maistre Hierosme aleander/preuost de saint Jehan de
Liege/prothonotaire τ bibliothecaire apostolique/en plusieurs
sciences τ langues excellent/expres nōtre τ orateur de sa saincte-
te τ dudit siege apostolique/enuoye specialement pource aff-
faire. Nous feist benignemēt presenter comme au vray deffen-
seur τ protecteur de la saincte foy catholique/aduocat et filz de
nostre mere saincte eglise/Nous requerāt que par tout noz terres τ seigneuries cōme roy catholique τ fidele voulsissions bail-
ler la main forte et bras seculier pour lexecution effectuelle de
toutes τ chascune les choses contēnees es lettres τ bulles apostoliques dessusdictes. ¶Apres lesquelles admōnitiōs τ pater-
nelles exhortations faictes audit Martin par nostredit sainct
pere le pape/vocation/citation/obligation τ condānation dicel-
luy τ de ses oeuures/ensēble la presentation des dessusdictes bulles a nous faicte τ diuulgation dicelles quasi par tout nostre re-
gne de la Germanie/τ par nostre cōmandemēt executee en noz.
pays dembas/τ mesnemēt en nostre ville de Louain/τ aussi es.
citez imperialles de Couloigne/de Mayance/de Treues et de
Liege/ledit Martin non seulemēt nest reuenu a vraye cōgnois
sance/penitence τ obedience de nostre mere saincte eglise et reuo-
cation de ses erreurs/mais cōme hōme plain de mauuaistie et
de fureur contre nostre foy et contre nostre mere saincte Eglise
voulant de plus en plus multiplier la detestable τ peruerse doctrine de son mauuais τ pernicieux engin/a fait tant en latin cō

He declared that those books, in whatever language they are written, would have to be burned and taken out of the people's memory forever.

As far as the said Martin is concerned, if he would not admit that he was wrong and repent, recognizing his mistakes in a given period of time, he would be declared disobedient, child of iniquity, and heretic. As such, he would have to be arrested, and, consistent with the ordinance and the rights, he would have to be punished according to the contents of the apostolic bulls. The honorable master Hieronymus Aleander, provost of Saint John of Liège, protonotary and librarian in several sciences and languages, nuncio and orator of the apostolic see, was sent especially for this matter, and, acting as a lawyer for our Holy Mother Church, he asked us to help in the execution of all the things contained in the letters and bulls of the apostolic see, as mentioned above.

After the fatherly admonitions and exhortations made to the said Martin by our Holy Father the pope; after the vocation, citation, obligation, and condemnation of Luther and his works; after the presentation of the bulls to us and their disclosure throughout almost all of Germany, and by our order executed in our Netherlands, our city of Louvain, and the imperial cities of Cologne, Mainz, Trier, and Liège, the said Martin Luther has not only refused to repent, return to the obedience of our Holy Church and renounce his errors, but this man of wickedness and furor against our faith and against our Mother Church wants to continue spreading the detestable and perverse doctrines of his wicked and pernicious spirit. He has written, in Latin

me en alemand plusieurs liures remplis de toutes anciènes er
reurs/heresies & blasphemes que ia par auant sont estez condã/
nez par les sacrez concilles & leglise catholique & apostolique:
& de iour en iour escript & diuulgue aultres nouueaulx erreurs
au grant scandale du peuple. ¶Esquelz liures il confond/vil/
laine & destruit lordre & lusaige des sept sainctz sacremens de le
glise par tant de temps inuiolablement & deuotement obseruez

¶Item il change& deshõnestemẽt infecte les inuiolables loix
du saint sacrement de mariage.

¶Item la maniere de receuoir le saint sacremẽt de lautel que
toute eglise obserue il veult reduyre a lusaige des dãnez scisma
tiques de borsme.

¶Item la confession sacramentalle qui est salutaire aux po/
ures ames pecheresses/il enuelopa du cõmencement de sorte q̃l
en fist de confession vne confusion. Et apres il arracha grant
partie dicelle. Et qui est plus a plourer ledit Martin menasse
en sesditz liures de dire plusieurs aultres choses dicelle cõfessiõ/
tellement que aucuns (cõme sommes aduertis) ont cõmence fai
re doubte de ladicte confession. Aucuns sont cõfessez imparfai/
ctement:& aultres que pis est ont laisse de eulx confesser du tout
Et ont ose publiquement conseiller aux aultres qui nestoit be/
soing soy confesser.

¶Item Et quant au sacre ordre de prestrisse par lequel se con/
sacre le precieux corps & sang de nostreseigneur.& aussi la puissã
ce & auctorite des clefz de nostre mere saincte eglise/non seulemẽt
il mesprise & dit estre cõmune a tout chascun lay/enfant & fẽmes
Mais encores il prouocque les seculiers a lauer leurs mains
dedans le sang des prestres.

¶Item le vicaire de dieu en terre nostre saint pere le pape vray
successeur de saint Pierre il appelle par noms & tiltres infames
Et persecute par inuectiues non accoustumez destre ouyes.et
blasphemes detestables.

¶Item il afferme quilny a point franc arbitre.mais cõme dit

and German, several books full of heresy and blasphemy which have been condemned by the sacred councils of the Catholic Church. Day after day he continues to write and spread new errors and false doctrines, to the great scandal of the people. In his books he confuses and destroys the order of the seven sacraments of the church, which for a long time have been invariably and devoutly observed.

Item. He changes and dishonestly infects the inviolable laws of the sacred sacrament of marriage.

Item. Regarding the manner of receiving the holy sacrament of the altar, which is observed by all churches: he wants to perform it as do the damned heretics of Bohemia.[65]

Item. As for the sacramental confession, which is beneficial to all poor sinning souls: he has made confusion of this confession, and afterwards he has turned it to his personal gain. What is even worse is that the said Martin threatens in his books to say many other things about this confession, so that some people already start to doubt. Many are confessed in the wrong manner; and even worse, some are allowed to confess everything about themselves while others are publicly advised that confession is not necessary at all.

Item. As for the holy order of the priesthood (through which the precious body and blood of our Lord is consecrated) and the power and authority of the keys of our Holy Mother Church: not only does Luther despise them by saying that they are common to all men, children, and women, but in addition, he provokes the seculars to wash their hands in the blood of the priests.

Item. The vicar of God here upon the earth, our Holy Father the pope, the true successor of Saint Peter, is called several infamous names by Luther. The pope is also blasphemed and persecuted.

Item. He says that there is no such thing as freedom of

---

65. The main feature of the Hussite observance of the Holy Eucharist was communion in both kinds (wafer and wine), or "under both species" (*sub utraque specie*). Roman Catholic practice since the twelfth century had been to withhold the chalice from the laity. The Hussites reinstituted the practice of allowing them both bread and wine. This in itself was not heresy, but what made it so was the Hussite belief that communion under both species was essential to salvation and that single communion, as practiced by the Roman church, was incomplete and did not contribute to salvation. The largest branch of the Hussite movement was known as the "Utraquists."

le poete.toutes choses viennent par necessite.

¶ Item il dit que la sacree messe ne profite ne a mors ne a vifz si non a cestuy qui la dit. Reprouuant lobseruation des ieunes. ¶ de prier dieu que leglise iusques icy a garde ¶ obserue.

¶ Item Du purgatoire ¶ des messes ¶ prieres ῷ nous faissons pour les ames des trespassez.¶ aussi des suffrages¶ pardõs de nostre mere saincte eglise il ne tient pas la vraye opinion dicelle eglise.mais celle des heretiques vauldoys ¶ vigleßtes.

¶ Item de leglise catholique il consent aux pelagians ¶ dessus ditz vigleßtes heretiques.

¶ Item il deprise ¶ contẽpne les doctrines et auctoritez que les saintz docteurs qui noꝰ ont precede nous ont luisseẽs pour nostre instruction/¶ diminue du tout son pouoir la deuotion que lon a aux sainctz

¶ Item il dit quil ny a point de superiorite ny dobedience.¶ destruit toute ciuile police ¶ ordre hierarchique ¶ ecclesiastique afin que les peuples soyent prouocquez a faire rebellion contre leurs superieurs tant spirituelz que tẽporelz.¶ se adõnent a tuer desrober ¶ mettre tout a feu ¶ a sang a la grande¶ manifeste ruyne de la chose publique ¶ crestiẽne.Et que pis est instituãt vne maniere de viure en laquelle chascun face ce que bon luy semblera a limitation des bestes brutes.¶ cõme hõme viuant sans loy.condãne ¶ deteste toutes loix ciuiles ¶ canoniques. tellemẽt que par presumption excessiue a brusle publiquemẽt les decretz ¶ decretales.¶(cõme dignement est a presumer)eust aussi brusle les loix ciuiles imperiales si neust eu plus de crainte de nostre glaiue imperial¶ royal qui na eu de lexcõmunication apostolique. ¶Et apres il na point honte de detracter ¶ mesdire des sacrez ¶ sainctz concilles generaulx.Et entre iceulx principalement destruit(autant que en luy est)le sainct concille de cõstãce/leῴl a ꝓpetuelle memoire ¶ gloire de la nation germaniῴ et aultres dõna fin aux scismes/et rendit la paix a nostre mere saincte eglise de telle sorte que la bouche pottue dudit Luther en

the will, but says, as does the poet, that all things are pre-determined.

Item. He says that the sacred mass does not benefit anybody except the one who says it, and in this way he stops the young people from the practice of praying to God, which the church has until now kept and observed.

Item. Regarding purgatory and the masses and prayers said for the souls of our dead, and also the suffrages and forgivings of our Holy Mother Church: he agrees, not with our church opinion, but with that of the Waldensian[66] and Wycliffite[67] heresies.

Item. As for the Catholic Church: he heeds the words of the Pelagians[68] and the heretical Wycliffites mentioned above.

Item. He despises and condemns the doctrines and authorities which the holy doctors preceding us have left for our instructions, and he degrades with all his might the devotion that we have for our saints.

Item. He says that there are no such things as superiority and obedience. He destroys all civil police and hierarchical and ecclesiastical order, so that people are led to rebel against their superiors, spiritual and temporal, and to start killing, stealing, and burning, to the great loss and ruin of public and Christian good. Furthermore, he institutes a way of life by which people do whatever they please, like beasts. They behave like men living without any law, condemning and despising all civil and canon laws to the extent that Luther, by excessive presumption, has publicly burned the decretals and (as we might expect) would have burned the imperial civil law had he not had more fear of the imperial and royal swords than he had of apostolic excommunication.

Furthermore, he is not ashamed to detract from and speak evil of the sacred and holy general councils. Among these he has primarily destroyed (as much as he was able to) the holy Council of Constance, which was convened for the glory and the memory of the German nation to put an end to the schism and to bring back peace to our Holy Mother Church.[69] The said Luther's polluted mouth, despising and

---

66. Beginning in the twelfth century, the Waldensians protested against the splendor and outward display of the medieval church. They made extreme poverty a prominent feature of their lives and anticlericalism one of their characteristics. They formed a lay

desprisant ꞇ annichilant icelluy concille/ scandalize luniuerselle
eglise. Et veult deshõnozer toute la crestiente appellant icelluy
concile la synagogue de Sathan.ꞇ affermant tous ceulx qui la
estoiët(cestassauoir Sigismund de eureuse memoire empereur
ꞇ les princes du saint empire)estre antecristz ꞇ apostres de lãte
crist homicides ꞇ pharisees.pource que au cõmandement dudit
saint concile feirent bzusler Jehan hus heretique. Adioustant
que tous les articles dudit Jehan hus condãnez audit concile
cõme erronez ꞇ heretiques sont euangeliques ꞇ crestiens.lesq̃lz
il veult deffendze ꞇ appzouuer. Et ceulx qui furent appzouuez
par le concile il reiecte ꞇ reffuse. Pzotestant cõme enraige que si
Jehan hus estoit vne foys heretique il pzêt pour gloire destre
dix foys plus heretiq̃.Et est si couuoiteux de nouuelletez. Voi
re de la humaine perdition que il na quasi escript chose (quelque
apparence de verite quelle ait)qui ne contiêne en soy quelque
pestilence ou esguillon de mozt.sans ses aultres liures remplis
de blaspħemes.erreurs ꞇ heresies qui ne sont poit dignes destre
nõmez par bouche de bon crestien.lesquelz on peult biẽ dire q̃
tãt de venin contiênent en soy que de motz. Et pour mettre
fin a lexpzession de erreurs dudit Martin.lesquelz a la verite
sont sans fin ꞇ sans nombze.il semble que ceste persõne de Mar
tin ne soit point hõme.mais vng diable soubz lespece dung hõ
me couuert de labillement dung religieux pour plus facilemẽt
mettre a la mozt eternelle lhumain lignage.Voulant assembler
les heresies de plusieurs heretiques par cy deuant condãnez et
expcõmuniez.ꞇ de long temps iusques en enfer enseuelis. Et y
adiouster aulcunes heresies par luy nouuellement expcogitees
pour en faire vne source ꞇ receptacle de toute iniquite.puanteur
ꞇ ozdure a la destruction de la foy catholique. Et soubz espece
de pzedicateur euãgelique il labeure detroubler ꞇ ãnichiler tou
te la paix ꞇ charite euangelique.tout ozdze et direction des cho
ses de ce monde.Et finablement de villenner et deshõnozer tou
te la beaulte de la face de nostre mere saincte eglise. Lesq̃lles

demolishing these, has scandalized the Universal Church. He wants to bring dishonor upon all of Christendom by calling this council "Satan's Synagogue" and by insulting all those who attended it, namely, "Sigismund of curious memory, emperor; and the princes of the Holy Empire, antichrists and apostles of the antichrist, murderers and pharisees," because, following an order from that council, they burned the heretic John Hus. Luther also added that all John Hus's articles, condemned during the council as wrong and heretical, were evangelical and Christian, and he wanted to defend him and approve of what he did. But he rejects and refuses whatever articles were approved by the council, protesting like a madman that if John Hus was once heretic, he [Luther] is proud to be ten times more heretic. And he seeks so much after new things, to the perdition of mankind, that he has not written anything (however truthful it may appear) that does not contain pestilences or the sting of death. This without mentioning the other books full of blasphemies, errors, and heresies not even worthy of mention by the mouth of a good Christian. These books contain as much poison as they have words.

To put an end to the numberless and endless errors of the said Martin, let us say that it seems that this man, Martin, is not a man but a demon in the appearance of a man, clothed in religious habit to be better able to deceive mankind, and wanting to gather the heresies of several heretics who have already been condemned, excommunicated, and buried in hell for a long time. Let us add to this all the heresies recently brought in by him to be the source of all iniquity and rubbish and to destroy the Catholic faith. As an evangelical preacher he labors to trouble and demolish all religious peace and charity and all order and direction in the things of this world. And finally, he brings dishonor upon all the beauty of our Holy Mother Church.

The death of John Hus. From the fifteenth-century Richental Chronicle.

ministry in some areas and went about the countryside reviving the practice of preaching. They denied the existence of purgatory and rejected the practice of indulgences and prayers for the dead. They were banned from the empire in 1253, although small sects of Waldensians continued to survive in the Piedmont and Briançonnais valleys and elsewhere.

67. This was the major heresy of the fourteenth century, originating in England with John Wyclif's criticisms of the doctrine of transubstantiation. Wyclif also attempted to reform the Roman church with an attack on the wealth of the clergy and church ownership of property. He and his followers disputed the authority of the church, claiming that the secular ruler had power over the ec-

choſes par nous τ les conſeilz des natiõs a nous ſubgectes diſ
ligément conſiderees/τ meſmement no⁹ requerant ſi affectueu
ſement en ceſt affaire icelluy noſtre ſaint pere le pape ſommes
deliberez de tout noſtre pouoir aſſiſter τ dõner ozdze pour eſtai
bze τ epterminer du tout ceſte dangereuſe τ moztelle hereſie. Et
pour plus meurement pzoceder entelle matiere auons ſouuent
appelle en noſtre pzeſence gens doctes et ſauans tant eccleſiaꝗ
ſtiques que ſeculiers/τ generallement tous eſtatz aſſemzlez en
gros nombze a la iournee celebzee par noſtre ozdõnance en ceꝰ
ſte noſtre cite de Bozmes/et par laduis de noſtredit conſeil et
pluſieurs aultres pzinces et pzelatz de noſdictes terres pays et
ſelgneuries/et aultres bões perſonnaiges eſtans en noſtre cõꝰ
paignie/finablement ſommes Venus a la concluſion ꝗ ſenſuit.
℘Aſſauoir/iacoit que Vng hõme cõme ledit Luther deſia conꝰ
damne et tendurcy en ſon obſtinee peruerſite/ſepare de la manie
re de Viure des creſtiens et notoire heretique ne ſoit ſelon les
dzoitz receuable pour le ouyz ou interroguer.touteſfoys pour
oſter toutes occaſions de maligner a ceulp qui fauoz-iſent ledit
Luther et ſeꝰdictes erreurs. Et psource que pluſieurs affermoiſꝰ
ent aucuns liures intitulez audit Martin luther nõ auoir eſte
compoſez ou eſcriptz par lup/et que aucuns aultres diſoiẽt nõ
deuoir pzoceder contre lup que ne euſſions pzemieremẽt oup ce
quil ſcautoit ou Vouldzoit dire. Auons par noz lettres patenꝰ
tes mande ſedit Luther quil Vint deuers no⁹ lup baillãt ſaulfꝝ
condupt et le faiſant accompaigner par lung de noz rops darꝝ
mes nõme alemaigne a ce par no⁹ enuoye Vers lup. Nõ pour
Vouloir iuger ou determier des merites de ceſte cauſe ne moiꝰ
pour Vouloir parmettre que les choſes qui concernent la ſainꝰ
cte foy catholique depuis ſi long temps par nouuelles diſputaꝰ
tions ſoient tirees en aucune controuerſie au grant ſcandalle et
peril du peuple creſtien et irriſion des infideles ennemps de noꝰ
ſtredicte ſaincte foy.Mais pour Veoir ſe par bões admonitiꝰ
ons ſedit Luther ſe Vouldzoit conuertir. ℘Pour ce comparant
B.i.

After having mentioned all these things before the council of the nations and our Holy Father the pope, we are endowed with all power to assist and give orders to put an end to and exterminate forever this dangerous and mortal heresy. To proceed better in this matter we appealed to learned people, both ecclesiastical and secular, and to all the general estates assembled in great number during the day designated by our ordinance, in this city of Worms. Upon the advice of our council, several other princes and prelates from our lands and domains and other good people of our company are also in attendance. We have finally arrived at the following conclusion.

Namely, that a man like the said Luther, already condemned and still persisting in his obstinate perversity, separated from the way of life of Christians, and a notorious heretic, should not be listened to nor questioned, according to the law, in order to prevent every opportunity for those who favor the said Luther and his errors to do evil. Because among the many titles bearing the name of Martin Luther some of the books may not have been composed or written by him and because several people said that proceedings should not be taken against him without first having heard what he knew, or what he would tell, we asked by letter patent that the said Luther come before us, giving him safe-conduct and having him escorted by one of our kings-of-arms from Germany, who was sent by us.[70] We asked him to come here, not to judge him or to praise his merits, nor to desire that the things concerning the holy Catholic faith — which for so long, because of new disputations, have brought great scandal and peril to Christians and have brought laughs from the unfaithful enemies of our holy faith — be further discussed, but to see if through good admonitions the said Luther could not be converted.

clesiastical and could confiscate the lands or benifices of unworthy clergymen. They also placed a very high value on the Bible as the only rule of faith.

68. This heresy, which arose during the late fourth and early fifth centuries, was based on the teachings of the British monk, Pelagius, who taught that the human will is completely free and equally ready to do good or evil. Pelagians believed that through his free will, man could take the initial steps toward salvation by his own efforts, apart from the assistance of God. Pelagius denied what came to be the orthodox doctrine of original sin, believing that Adam's transgression was a purely personal sin and could not cause

Imperial herald Kaspar Sturm. Sketch by Albrecht Dürer.

ledit Luther personnellemeut audit Vormes deuant nous et
esditz princes prelatz et tous aultres estas en ensuyut nostres
mandement lauons fait interroguer/premieremét si lauoit fait
ou non les liures lesquelz lup furent lors monstrez et intelligi-
blemét chascun diceulp par leurs tiltres denómez/et sil Vouloit
reuocquer le contenu esditz liures en ce qui estoit contre la foy
catholique/les sacrez concilles generaulp, decretz apostoliques
cerimonies de leglise. et louables coustumes obseruees et gar-
dees par noz predecesseurs et par nous iusques au iourdhup/
en sollicitant Vers ledit Luther tant en nostre nom que de tous
les assistans par diuerses monitions et ephortatiós ql Voul-
sist humblemént retourner a lunite et cómunion de nostre mere
saincte eglise. Et tellement sest lon porte pour redupre ledit Luther quil suffisoit assez pour lamollir et cóuertir sil neust este ph
dur que pierre. ¶Lequel Luther ce cógneut deuant nous et les
princes et estas dessusditz que les liures deuát lup nómez esto-
pent siens protestát qui ne les pourroit et ne Vouldroit iamais
nper. Et dauantaige dit que il en auoit encores cópose des aul
tres qui ne furét pour lors produitz a cause qui ne sont pas par-
uenus en noz mains. Et que quant a ce qui appartiét a reuoca
tion du contenu esditz liures il demandoit dilation lup estre dó
nee pour y penser. Laquelle combien que iustemét se deuoit des
nper attendu que les choses qui sont cótre la foy ne meritent di
lation. et q en nosdictes lettres euocatiues dudit Martin estoit
declaire la cause de sa citation affin quil pensast a la respóce ql
Vouldroit dóner en nostre presence/toutessops par clemence et
benignite de laquelle Voulons tousiours Vser lup fut octrope
le terme de Vingtquatre heures. Lesquelles passees comparás
de rechief ledit Luther deuát nous et lesditz princes et estas lup
furent de nostre part faictes plusieurs admonitions et ephorta
tions pour sa reduction et sauluement/lup promectát aussi que
sil Vouloit reuocquer le mal que dessus est dit nous procureri-
ons Vers nostre saint pere le pape quil seroit receu en grace/ et

For this reason the said Luther appeared here in Worms before us and before the princes, prelates, and other people from the several estates. Following our order, we had him questioned, asking him first if, yes or no, he had written the books which were then named and shown to him and [secondly] if he wanted to revoke the contents of these books concerning things against the Catholic faith, the sacred general councils, the apostolic decrees, and the church rites and customs observed and kept by our predecessors and by us down to the present day. We requested of the said Luther, both in our name and in that of all our assistants, that he be willing to return humbly to the unity and communion of our Mother Church. And even then it would have been easy to convert him and soften his heart if the said Luther had not been as obstinate as a rock.

Luther admitted before us and before the princes and the people of the diet that the books named were his and that he could not and would not ever deny them. Furthermore, he said that he has written others that were not shown here because they were not yet in our possession. As far as the revocation of the contents of his books was concerned, he asked that a delay be given him to think about it. This delay should have been refused: things that are against the faith do not deserve postponement. Moreover, because we mentioned in our letter to Luther the reason for his coming here, he should have had time enough to think about the answer he would give us. However, we were willing to give him a delay of twenty-four hours. After that time he was to be brought again before us and before the princes and the people of the diet. We also promised him that if he would revoke the evil mentioned above, we would arrange for him to have an interview with our Holy Father the pope. And also, after just and diligent deliberation, [we agreed

punishment to others. All people were thus born without sin, and infant baptism was unnecessary. His chief theological opponent was St. Augustine.

69. The Council of Constance (1414–17) was the most significant church assembly in many centuries. Its announced purposes were to reform the church in head and members, to combat heresy (particularly that of John Hus), and to heal the great schism. In the first two endeavors the council was only partially successful, but in the third it did succeed in deposing three popes and establishing its own appointee, Martin V, on the papal throne, thus ending forty years of schism between Rome and Avignon. It also declared the principle

ferions vers luy tant que par fidele iustice et diligente exami=
nation sily eust quelque bonne doctrine dedans ses liures lon
la departiroit de la mauuaise faisant côfermer la bône par lau=
ctorite apostolique. Mais ce non obstât par parolles ꝗ gestes
malauenans a vng religieux/ dit publiquement quil ne chan=
geroit vng seul mot de tout ce questoit contenu en ses liures ꝝ
Declairant en nostre presence ꝗ de tous les estas les decretz a=
postoliques et les saintz conciles generaulx auoit failly plusi=
eursffoys/et se contredire a soymesmes. et que quant a luy les te
noit pour friuoles et de nulle valeur/et quilne reuocqueroit au
cune chose de ce quil auoit escript iusques a ce que par raison a
soy euidente et par les auctoritez et parolles expresses de la sai=
cte escripture il fust conuaincu de telle sorte ꝗ sa conscience et sã
taisie fussent satisfaictes et contentes. Repetant souuentesfois
pour couurir ses faulsetez et astutes deceptiôs ꝗ il ne pourroit
sa côscience sauluer ꝗ chãger la parolle de dieu. Côme si no⁹ le
requerisions ꝗ il changeast la parolle de dieu/et non plustost ꝗ
selô la vraye parolle de dieu il se retiroit au giron de nostre me
re saincte eglise contre laꝗlle si villainement il sestoit rebelle.
Et affin ꝗ ledit Luther donnast côuenable fin a ses mauuais
actes en ceste iournee/et ce ꝗlauoit tresmal cômence il parache=
uast encores pis. Il ne sceust dissimuler le pernicieux couraige
ꝗlauoit/car en se resiouyssant de la destruction des crestiês les
quelz a raison de sa peruerse doctrine veolt en discort trouble ꝗ
diuision/il voulut ensuyuant la facon des heretiques peruertir
et malicieusement interpreter contre lintention de nostre saul=
ueur lauctorite du saint euâgile pour faire seruir en son mal ꝓ
pos. Assauoir la ou nostre redempteur dit. Je ne suis pas ve=
nu a mectre la paix mais le glaiue. Martin dit ꝗ semblablemêt
il ny a chose au monde a luy plus ioyeuse ꝗ veoir pour la paro
le de dieu suruenir parcialite et dissension. Côme adire par ses
nouuelles opinions lesꝗlles par faulx tiltre il couure de la pa
rolle de dieu. Il vouloit susciter parcialitez. dissensions. discorz

that] if there was any good in the contents of his books we would keep it and expurgate only the things contrary to our doctrines. Whatever was good would be confirmed and authorized by apostolic authority. Nevertheless, through evil words and gestures towards our priests, he publicly pronounced that he would not change one word of the contents of his books, declaring in our presence and in that of the diet that the apostolic decrees and the holy general councils contradicted each other more than once. As far as he was concerned, he did not hold these decrees and councils to be true, and he would not revoke one thing of what he had written until he was convinced otherwise by the Holy Scriptures or by divine authority. He repeated many times, to cover up his false doctrines, that he could not save his soul if he were to change one of God's words — as if we had asked him to change God's words! On the contrary, he had rebelled against our Holy Mother Church. Finally, the said Luther ended the day in an even worse manner than he had started it. He could not hide his pernicious audacity. He was rejoicing about the destruction of the Christians who, because of his doctrines and his perversity, were living in discord, trouble, and division. Luther also wanted, like the heretics, to pervert and interpret in an evil manner the authority of the holy gospel and to use it maliciously. (For example, where our Redeemer says, "I have not come to bring peace, but the sword," Martin says that there is no greater joy in the world for him than to see contention and factions because of the word of God.) In this manner does he cover up his new opinions concerning the word of God. He wanted to raise factionalism, dissension, discord, crimes,

---

of *conciliarism*, that is, the notion that the supreme ruling organ of the universal church was the general council, not the papacy. But during the next century conciliarism was gradually overcome by the vigorous countermeasures of several Renaissance popes impatient with the cumbersome ineffectiveness of the councils.

70. *King-of-arms* was the official designation of the imperial heralds. A similar title was attached to the principal heralds of the French and English kings. Kaspar Sturm was the king-of-arms sent to escort Luther from Wittenberg.

des.scismes.guerres et pilleries entre les crestiens côme nous
Voyons euidêment par effect et au grant dômaige du bien com
mun de la religion crestiêne eust on plus amplemêt apparceu
se la doctrine dudit Luther eust perseuere en sa Vigueur.
¶Ouye adoncqs par nous la responce dudit Luther tant ini-
que et infidele nous determinames lors de le renuoyer sans ar
rester ensupuant la forme de son saulfcondupt.Et subit proce-
deraux remedes iuridiqs en tel cas reqs et necessaires ainsi q̃
lon peult auoir congneu par nostre declaration surce faicte et
escripte de nostre propre main. Et le lendemain ensupuant de-
clairee aux princes et aultres estatz. Touteffoys encores a la
reqste des dessusditz des estatz en ensupuât la parolle de nostre
createur/disant quil ne Veult la mort du pecheur/mais quil se
conuertisse ⁊Viue.Dônasmes audit Luther troys iours de delay pour soy reuocquer ⁊ amender pendant lequel temps deux
electeurs/deux euesques/deux princes/⁊ deux deputez de noz ci
tez au nom de tous les estas icy assemblez firent appeller ledit
Luther par deuant eulx luy remonstrant quelz remedes nous
estions deliberez de trouuer ⁊ de qlle maniere/⁊ par qlles peines
nous Voulions proceder contre luy.Lesquelz firent aussi leurs
deuoirs par toutes Voyes sans riens laisser q̃ pourroit seruir
a la reduction dung hôme de redupre ledit Luther.Car auecqs
les labeurs ⁊ peines inutilement portees ⁊ prinses pour ce faire
il ne souffist encores a lung des electeurs a ce cômis/mais prit
auec luy deux docteurs lung en theologie et lautre en droit canon ⁊ ciuil de doctrine singuliere ⁊ Vie louable/⁊ de rechief icelluy electeur fist par lesditz docteurs faire telles remonstrances
audit Luther q̃ icelluy côme confus ne scauoit q̃ dire.Et depuis
encores ledit electeur entre les aultres remonstrances admone
sta icelluy Luther a part de retourner a lusaige ⁊ obseruâce ecclesiastique q̃ nostre saint pere le pape/le saint siege apostoliq/
nous⁊ tous estas ⁊ toutes fideles nations ont iusques a p̃sent
gardies ⁊ gardent plustost q̃ demourer en son opinion erronee

wars, and evil things among Christians, as we can readily see from the effects and the great damage to the common good of the Christian religion.

Thus enlightened by the wicked and unfaithful response of the said Luther, we decided to send him away without arresting him, in accord with the terms of his safe-conduct and the judicial procedures required in such cases, especially since they were written by us. The next day all of the princes and representatives of the various estates were informed of this decision. This was done at the request of the princes and the diet, according to our Creator's words when He said that He does not want the sinner's death but wants him to be converted and live. We gave Luther a three-day delay for him to repent. During that time, two electors, two bishops, two princes, and two deputies of our cities gathered here in the name of all the estates and had Luther present himself to be informed of our remedies and of the manner and type of punishment with which we would proceed against him if he did not repent. All of them did their duty without letting anyone do any harm to the said Luther. One of the electors made remonstrances to Luther to such an extent that Luther could not utter a word.[71] This elector even admonished Luther to stop being stubborn and to go back to the ecclesiastical obedience and customs that we, our Holy Father the pope, the Holy Apostolic See, all the diet, and all faithful nations have kept until now. He was promised that if he wanted to abandon this erroneous

Justus Jonas

---

71. This was Richard Greiffenklau, archbishop of Trier, a highly respected churchman, scholar, and imperial elector, who two years earlier had served as arbitrator between Luther and Miltitz prior to their Altenburg meeting. He was now chairman of the commission negotiating with Luther. In these discussions, Luther was permitted to be accompanied by three advisors of his own: his attorney, Hieronymus Schurff, and his close friends, the noted scholars, Nikilaus von Amsdorf and Justus Jonas.

de laqlle sil Bouloit departir z retourner a lobediance de ses su=
perieurs son honneur z son salut luy seroit garde/côme en cas se
blable a plusieurs des saintz peres q aultresfoys ont erre a este
fait z obserue.Ausquelles choses(côme nous reporterent lesdits
deputez)ledit Luther dôna responce non meilleure ql auoit fait
deuant.En disant q non seullement il auoit suspectz to⁹ z chas
cun de nous/mais q plus est si le concille general estoit assem=
ble ne se Bouldroit a icelluy soubzmettre.Et si côme Veritable=
ment sommes infoimez a ose dire de sa bouche posllue q les cho
ses de leu angile z de la foy catholiq iamais ne furent bien trai=
ctees es côcilles generaulx Et a la verite no⁹eust este matiere
de admiration côment icelluy Luther ayant appelle de la senté
ce de nostre saint pere le pape au concille general côme son der=
nier refuge/a tant de malz de iniure dit z escript des côcilles ge=
neraulx z a iceulx de toute sa puyssance z engin derogue et de=
traicte si ce ne fust q la coustume z maniere des heretiques est q
tout ainsi ql nest chose au monde quilz craingnent tant côme le
concille general/pareillement nest chose a iceulx tant propre et
appartenant côme a soymesmes côtredire tant en faitz q en ditz
z escriptz/ce procurant z promouât la diuine prouidéce Boulât
par ce destruyre z anichiler les temeraires z dânables inuêtiôs
des heretiques ennemys de Verite.Laqlle chose plus q en nul
aultre precedent heretiq est Verifiee z manifestee audit Luther
z en ses oeuures. ℂ Lesquelles choses dessusdictes ainsi faictes
z demenees z par nous z lesditz estas z aultres noz conseilliers
meuremêt z longuemêt côsiderees/attêdu q ledit Luther demou
roit si arreste z obstine en ses opinions/erreurs z heresies q les
gens prudens qui lauyient Veu z ouy le reputoient ou foicene/
ou possede de quelque maling esperit.Si le feismes rêuoyer z ac
compaigner par nostre dessusdit roy darmes a sa seurete selon
la teneur de son saulfconduit/ en luy assignant terme de Bingt
iours a côpter du.xxB.dauril du psent an/lequel iour se partit
de ceste cite de Bboimes.Et desmaintenant est bien iuste z ne=

opinion and return to obeying his superiors again, his honor and his salvation would be preserved, as had been done in the past for some of the holy fathers who had also been led astray. The said Luther gave no better response than he had previously given (according to the report of the deputies). He said that not only was he suspicious of each one of us, but that even if a general council were assembled, he still would not submit to it. And, if we were informed correctly, he even dared say with his polluted mouth that the things of the gospel and the Catholic faith have never been treated well by the general councils. Luther has appealed from the sentence of our Holy Father the pope to the general council as his last resort, even though he has said so many wicked and insulting things and has written such evil things about the general councils. With all his strength and ingenuity he has diverted and confused the people in the manner of the heretics who say there is nothing on earth they fear so much as the general councils. That is because the one thing done there, and that by divine providence, is to contradict the actions and writings of the heretics, enemies of truth, in order to destroy and annihilate their rash inventions. This [attitude towards the councils], more than any other heretical event, has been verified and manifested in Luther and his works.

The things mentioned above have been studied by us carefully and at length. Since the said Luther was so stubborn and obstinate in his opinions, errors, and heresies, the wise people who had seen and heard him said that he was mad and possessed by some evil spirit. We had him sent back, accompanied by our king-of-arms for his safety, according to the contents of his safe-conduct. We gave him a period of twenty days, beginning on the twenty-fifth of April of the present year, which was the day he left this city of Worms.[72] And now it is only just and necessary

72. The document is incorrect here, since Luther actually left Worms on April 26.

ceſſaire de pourueoir des remedes en tel cas côuenables/ce que
auons fait τ decerne en la maniere qui ſenſupt.

℘Premieremēt/a lhôneur de dieu tout puiſſant τ deue reueren
ce de ſon Vicaire en terre noſtre ſaint pere le pape τ du ſaint ſie
ge apoſtolique eſmeuz par le bon zele τ affectiô q̃ par noſtre na
turelle inclination et par imitation de noz predeceſſeurs auons
a la deffenſion de la foy catholique τ protection de la ſaicte egli
ſe rômaine pour y deſpendre noz biens τ employer noſtre puiſ/
ſance/ſeigneuries/amys τ ſubgetz/τ ſi beſoing eſt y eppoſer no/
ſtre Vie τ noſtre propre ſang τ tout tant quila pleu a dieu nous
dôner en cemonde/de lauctorite a noᵘ appartenãt eu ſur ce laꝺ/
uis deſditz princes/prelatz/cheualiers de noſtre orꝺre τ gens de
noſtre conſeilen gros nombre aſſemblez deuers nous orꝺônez
eſtre depeſchez mandatz en chaſcune de noz chancelleries τ ſei/
gneuries ſelon les langaiges diceulp de la ſuſtãce des preſentes
par leſquelles pour execution de la ſentence côtre ledit Luther
τ ſa faulſe doctrine condãnee par noſtre ſaint pere le pape Vray
τ legitime iuge en ceſte partie contenue es bulles deſſuſꝺictes a
nous preſentees/nous auons a perpetuelle memoire declaire et
decerne/declairons τ decernôs par ces preſentes tenir τ reputer
ledit Martin luther pour mēbre aliene pourry τ trãche hors du
corps de noſtre mere ſaicte egliſe côme obſtine ſciſmatique τ nos
toire heretique/τ pour tel le tenons τ reputons/τ par Voᵘτ chaſ
cun de Vous Voulons eſtre tenu τ repute. ℭΕt pource deffen/
dôs eppreſſemēt que nul ſoit ſi oſe ou harꝺy de doreſenauãt pre
ſumer receuoir τ deffendre/ſouſtenir ou fauoriſer par parole ou
par fait ledit Martin luther. Mais ſi peult eſtre reallement ap/
prehende Voulons que ainſi ſoit fait/τ quil ſoit puny incôtinãt
côme notoire heretique/ou quil ſoit perſônellemēt preſente par
deuant nous. Du pour le moins quil ſoit garde ſeurement tant
que ceſtuy ou ceulp qui laurons prins nous ayent de ce aduer/
tis/ et ayons mande la maniere de proceder oultre contre ledit
Martin. Εn quoy faiſant remunererons côdignemēt leur bon

to find remedies pertaining to such a case, which we have done and executed as follows.

First of all, to the honor of Almighty God, in reverence both to his vicar here on earth, our Holy Father the pope, and to the Holy Apostolic See, moved by zeal, affection, and our natural inclination, and in imitation of our predecessors, we appeal to the defense of the Catholic faith and to the protection of the Holy Roman Church. We desire to defend our goods, to use our power, our domains, our friends and subjects, and if necessary, to risk our own life and blood and whatever it pleases God to give us in this world. By the authority vested in us, and upon the advice of the princes, prelates, knights of our orders, and gentlemen of our council gathered here in great numbers, we have ordered that mandates be sent to every one of our chancelleries and domains in their own language by which the sentence is to be executed against Martin Luther and his false doctrine (already condemned by our Holy Father the pope, the true and legitimate judge in these matters), as contained in the above-mentioned bulls presented to us.[73] We have declared and hereby forever declare by this edict that the said Martin Luther is to be considered an estranged member, rotten and cut off from the body of our Holy Mother Church. He is an obstinate, schismatic heretic, and we want him to be considered as such by all of you.

For this reason we forbid anyone from this time forward to dare, either by words or by deeds, to receive, defend, sustain, or favor the said Martin Luther. On the contrary, we want him to be apprehended and punished as a notorious heretic, as he deserves, to be brought personally before us, or to be securely guarded until those who have captured him inform us, whereupon we will order the appropriate manner of proceeding against the said Luther.

Woodcut from a 1521 pamphlet describing the indulgence trade.

---

73. Both *Exsurge Domine* and *Decet Romanum* were in the emperor's possession by the time he signed the edict, and it is to these that he referred in this passage; but *Decet Romanum* had not yet been published.

seruice/τ ferons satisfaire tous les despens au contentement de
cestuy ou ceulx quil appartiendra. ¶Et quant aux complices ad￾herans/receuans τ en quelque maniere audit Martin fauori￾sans ou imitateurs de sa doctrine silz se meslent plus dudit Lu
ther eulx demonstrans obstinez en leurs peruersitez/τ quilz na
pent obtenu absolution du pape des censures τ maulx par eulx
encourus τ comis a son occasion Voulons estre procede contre
iceulx τ tous τ chascuns leurs biès meubles et immeubles par
les iuges ordinaires des lieux ou ilz serot/ou par noz parlemès
τ conseilz/tant de malines come aultres auxquelz la congnoissà
ce en deura appartenir selon que aux accusateurs et denoncia￾teurs ou noz procureurs fiscaulx semblera bon/ le tout selon et
ensupuant les costitutions τ loix tant ciuiles/canoniques q̃ di￾uines faictes τ ordonees cotre ceulx qui comettent heresies ou
crime de lese maieste/tellemèt que a linstance τ requeste de quel
conque persone que ce puist estre soit procede contre tous τ chas
cuns de quelque degre/dignite/ou priuilege quilz soient. contre
uenàs ou desobeissans a cestuy nostre present edit en quelq̃ ma
niere que ce soit. ¶Item Voulons que les biens des delinquàs
qui de droit ou en vertu dicellup nostre present edit seront cofi￾squez soient appliquez pour la moitie a nous τ pour lautre aux
accusateurs ou denonciateurs desditz delinquàs. ¶Aussi Vou
lons que noz procureurs fiscaulx au cas quilz neussent accusa￾teurs facent proceder contre lesditz delinquans par inquisition
en nostre nom τ instance. Et en cas quil y ait accusateurs Vou
lons quilz se ioingnent auec eulx ou nom de nostre fisque pour
nostre droit et interest. Sans que en ce aucuns empeschemens
leur soit fait ou donne. ¶Item nous Vous mandons τ coman￾dons aussi respectiuement chascun en sop τ si come a lup appar￾tiendra que a son de trompe faciez euocquer des quattre quar￾tiers des lieux ou villes esquelles se publiera ce present edit le
peuple pour comparoir au lieu auquel on a accoustume de pu￾blier noz editz et mandemens τ illecq̃s faictes lire de mot a mot

Those who will help in his capture will be rewarded generously for their good work.

As for his accomplices, those who help or favor the said Martin in whatever manner or who show obstinacy in their perversity, not receiving absolution from the pope for the evils they have committed, we will also proceed against them and will take all of their goods and belongings, movable and fixed, with the help either of the judges in the area in which they reside or of our parliaments and councils at Malines or in other cities in which these events are made known.[74] Action will be taken according to the desire of the accusers or of our fiscal procurators, but always according to the constitution and the laws, whether canon, civil, or divine, written against those who commit heresy or the crime of *lèse majesté*. These laws will be applied regardless of person, degree, or privilege if anyone does not obey our edict in every manner.

Item. We desire that the goods of delinquents that might be confiscated according to this edict be divided, one half going to us and the other half to the accusers and denouncers.

We also desire that where there are no accusers our fiscal procurators proceed against the delinquents through inquisition in our name. And if there are accusers, we want them to join you, in the name of our fiscals, for our right and interest, without any opposition given to them.

Item. We ask you and command that "with the sounding of the trumpet" you call the people from the four corners of the villages and cities where this edict will be published and gather them where it is customary to publish our edicts and mandates. You will then read this edict word for word and

---

74. Malines was the administrative and financial center of the Burgundian empire until the death of Charles the Bold in 1477. In 1496 the *Chambres des Comptes* of Lille, Brussels, and the Hague were all reunited at Malines, and in 1504 the Burgundian high court (*Grand Conseil*) was created and established there by Charles's father, Philip I. This centralization was cut short by Philip's death, but Malines continued to occupy a primary role in the legal administration of Charles's territories.

a haulte et intelligible voix ce present edit. En cōmandant sur les peines en cellup edit cōtenus qui soit garde ⁊ obserue tout le cōtenu en icellup/⁊ faissāt expressemēt deffēdre de nostre part sur les peines dessusdictes que nul de ꝗlque auctorite/ degre ou priuilege quil puist estre soit si ose ou hardp de achepter/vēdre/tenir/lire/escrire ou faire escrire/imprimer ou faire imprimer/ affermer/soustenir ou deffendre aucūs des liures/ escriptures ou opinions dudit Martin luther cōtenues esditz liures ⁊ escriptures dicellup Luther/tant en Alemand/latin/flamand que ꝗlcōꝗ auꝶtre langue/tāt de ceulp ꝗ sont condānez par nostre sait pere cōme aultres ꝗlconques ia composez ou que si apres se pourront composer par icellup Luther ou ses disciples ⁊ fauteurs en ꝗlque sorte ⁊ maniere que puisse estre. Cōbien ꝗl p auroit esditz liures aucunes doctrines catholicꝗ meslees⁊ entrelassees pour plus facilement deceuoir ⁊ tromper les simples personnes Ce non obstant voulons lesditz liures vniuersellemēt estre prohibez deffendus ⁊ bruslez ⁊ du tout abolis. En quop faisāt oultre la iuste epecution de ladicte sentence du saint siege apostolique nous ensupuons la treslouable ordōnance ⁊ coustume des anciēs bons crestiens qui firent brusler ⁊ ānichiler les liures des heretiques cōme Arrians/Priscilliantzes Nestoriens/Eutpchiens ⁊ aultres/⁊ tout le cōtenu dicculpsliares tant le bien que le mal ce qui est bien⁊ deuemēt fait. Car si lon doit interdite ou deffendre la viande ou il p a vne seule goutte de venin pour dāgier de linfection corporelle dautant plus fault il regetter la doctrine(ꝗlque bōne quelle soit)laquelle enuelupe auec sop le venī de heresie ou erreur qui infecte/corrōpt et destruit soubz vmbre de charite tout ce qui p peult estre de bon au grant peril et dāgier des ames. ¶Et pourtant voulons⁊ voꝰ mandons a voꝰ ⁊ chascuȵ de vous apans administration de iustice ꝗ auec toute cure ⁊ diligence effectuelle incōtinant cestes veues faictes brusler ⁊ destrupre public quement tous ⁊ chascuns les liures dudit Luther tant en Alemand/flamand/latin ꝗ aulcre langue escriptz

with a loud voice. We order, upon the penalties contained herein, that the contents of this edict be kept and observed in their entirety; and we forbid anyone, regardless of his authority or privilege, to dare to buy, sell, keep, read, write, or have somebody write, print or have printed, or affirm or defend the books, writings, or opinions of the said Martin Luther, or anything contained in these books and writings, whether in German, Latin, Flemish, or any other language. This applies also to all those writings condemned by our Holy Father the pope and to any other book written by Luther or any of his disciples, in whatever manner, even if there is Catholic doctrine mixed in to deceive the common people. For this reason we want all of Luther's books to be universally prohibited and forbidden, and we also want them to be burned. We execute the sentence of the Holy Apostolic See, and we follow the very praiseworthy ordinance and custom of the good Christians of old who had the books of heretics like the Arians,[75] Priscillians,[76] Nestorians,[77] Eutychians,[78] and others burned and annihilated, even everything that was contained in these books, whether good or bad. This is well done, since if we are not allowed to eat meat containing just one drop of poison because of the danger of bodily infection, then we surely should leave out every doctrine (even if it is good) which has in it the poison of heresy and error, which infects and corrupts and destroys under the cover of charity everything that is good, to the great peril of the soul.

Therefore, we ask you who are in charge of judicial administration to have all of Luther's books and writings burned and destroyed in public, whether these writings are in German, Flemish, Latin, or in any other written language

Contemporary woodcut of sixteenth-century printing press.

---

75. The Arian heresy was named for Arius, a priest in Alexandria in the early fourth century who taught a doctrine of the Trinity which subordinated the Son (*Logos*) to the Father to the point of denying the divinity of Christ. Jesus was not coeternal with God, because he had been created by God and, therefore, did not always exist. Only God is without beginning. This doctrine was condemned at the Council of Nicaea in A.D. 325.

76. The Priscillian heresy was a mystical movement that originated in Spain in the fourth century. It denied the necessity of earthly organizations, including the church. Salvation could be found outside the visible church. In view of the role prophecy had played in early Christian history, the Priscillians felt that inspiration was all that was really necessary.

ou a escrire/tant par luy que ses disciples/ou imitateurs de sa
faulse doctrine/heretiq̃/sismatique/Voye et source de toute per
uersite et inquietation. En donnant faueur/ayde/et assistance
feablement et effectuellement aux messaigiers de nostre sainct
pere le Pape toulessoys et quantes que par iceulp ou leurs de
putez serez requis. Et neaumoins en leurs absences faictes par
Vous mesmes publiquement bzusler lesdis liures/ et executer
les aultres choses comme dessus est dict. Et a cest effect mã
dons ⁊ expressement ozdonnons a tous noz subgectz des lieux
de Vostre Juridiciõ sur les peines dessusdictes de en ce et leurs
deppẽdances Vous assister et obeyz cõme a nostre ppze psonne.
ET POVR ce que a toute diligence fault pouruecit que
les ditz liures du dit Martin Luther/ ou la doctrine diceulp
liures tiree soubz le nom et tiltre de quelque aultre aucteur ne
soient multipliez ⁊ publiez. ET aussi pource que iournellemẽt
plusieurs liures se composent et impziment plains de mauuai
ses doctrines et exemples. Et affin que lennemy de humaine
nature par toute astuce attrape les pouures ames des Chzesti
ens se diuulguent aussi painctures et pmages desraisonnables
par lesquelx tant liures que pmages les Chzestiens tombent
en tresgrans erreurs en la foy et bõnes meurs/et non seullemẽt
scandales et haynnes immoztelles a loccasion de ce (cõme ap
pert par experience) sont sozties et engendzees. Mais aussi de
iour en iour et de plus en plus seditions/ scismes/rebellions/et
cõmotions sont apparans de suruenir es Royaulmes/pzouin
ces/citez/et Villes de la Chzestiente/cõme il est fozt a craindze.
Pour ceste Cause affin de estaindze ceste peste tant moztel
le mandons et cõmandons que nul soit si ose ne hardy de doze
sennauant cõposer/escrire/impzimer/ paindze/ Vendze/ acheter/
auoir, ou faire impzimer/escrire/Vendze/ou paindze en quelque
sozte que ce soit telle maniere de liures pestilencieux ou diffa
matoires/ Inuectibles/ escriptures/ ou pmages contenantes
aulcun deshonneur/oppzobze/ou quelq̃ erreur/ ou article repu
L.i.

and whether they are written by himself, his disciples, or the imitators of his false and heretical doctrines, which are the source of all perversity and iniquity. Moreover, we ask you to help and assist the messengers of our Holy Pope. In their absence you will have all those books publicly burned and execute all the things mentioned above.

To that effect, we ask and require all our subjects of your jurisdiction to consider the penalties herein mentioned, and we also ask them to assist and obey you as they would obey us.

We also have to be careful that the books or the doctrines of the said Martin Luther not be written and published under other authors' names. Daily, several books full of evil doctrine and bad examples are being written and published. There are also many pictures and illustrations circulated so that the enemy of human nature, through various tricks, might capture the souls of Christians. Because of these books and unreasonable pictures, Christians fall into transgression and start doubting their own faith and customs, thus causing scandals and hatreds. From day to day, and more and more, rebellions, divisions, and dissensions are taking place in this kingdom and in all the provinces and cities of Christendom. This is much to be feared.

For this reason, and to kill this mortal pestilence, we ask and require that no one dare to compose, write, print, paint, sell, buy, or have printed, written, sold, or painted, from now on in whatever manner such pernicious articles so

---

77. The Nestorian heresy arose out of an attempt by Nestorius, Patriarch of Constantinople (d. *ca*. A.D. 451), to combat the Arian heresy. Nestorius claimed that Christ had two natures: one was human and had been created; the other was divine and coeternal with God. Therefore, Christ was both human and divine at the same time. The human Jesus could sin, whereas the God Christ could not. Nestorians went further and claimed that Mary was not the mother of Jesus Christ the god, but only of Jesus Christ the man. Christ's divine nature joined with his human nature only after his birth. Nestorianism was condemned by the Council of Ephesus in A.D. 431.

78. A further complication in the dilemma of Christ's nature came with the doctrine of *monophysitism,* which developed in opposition to Nestorianism. It held that the union of the divine *Logos* (Son of God) with human nature resulted in the absorption of the humanity into the divinity. Christ, therefore, had a single divine nature only. Monophysitism was condemned at Chalcedon in A.D. 451 but continued to flourish in Egypt and in the Middle East. The

gnant a la saincte foy orthodoxe/ou a ce que leglise Chatholi=
que et Apostolique a garde ꝓ obserue iusques a present. Ou au
blasme et diffame du sainct pere/prelatz deglise et Princes secu
lie rs/Estudes generaulx/ou facultez desdictz Estudes/ꝗ aul=
tres hõnestes personnes tant cõstituez en auctorite cõme priuez
Et generalement quelꝗ chose indue non concordante a bonnes
meurs/a la saincte eglise Rõmaine/et au bien publiꝗ crestien.
ꝶ Et au surplus Voulons/ ꝗ apres la publicacion du present
edict soyent publiquement prins et bruslez tous et chescuns
liures/escriptures diffamatoires/ inuectiues/ ou ymages de la
forme dessusdicte que se pourront trouuer par my noz pays /
soubz le nom de quelꝗ aucteur qui soit ou ꝗ cy apres pourroient
estre imprimez/escriptz/ou compilez en quelque maniere de lan
gaige que ce puist estre. ꝶ Et faictes auec soigneuse diligence
apprehender au corps ꝗ biens realemẽt ꝗ de fait tous ceulx qui
deuement Vous apparoistrõt estre rebelles a noz ordõnances
dessusdictes en les punyssãt par lexecution des peines cy deuãt
exprimees ꝗ ordõnees par droit tant diuin canonique que ciuil
ꝶ Et affin de oster occasion que le Venin de faulse doctrine et
mauuais exemple ne soit respandu par la crestiente et que lex=
cellent artifice de imprimer liures soit seulement exerce en bons
ꝗ louables Vsaiges. eu sur ce meur conseil et deliberation Vou=
lons ꝗ de nostre auctorite mandons ꝗ cõmandons par ce pjent
edit lequel Voulons ꝗ decernons obtenir auctorite de loy inuio
lable et perpetuelle ꝗ doresenauant sur peine de confiscation de
corps ꝗ de biens nul libraire ou imprimeur ou aultre ꝗlconque
soit si ose ne hardy de imprimer ou faire imprimer en ꝗlque lieu
que ce soit aucuns liures ou aultres escriptures ꝗlconqu es esꝗl
les soit faicte mentionde la saincte escripture ou interpretation
dicelle(ꝗlque peu que ce soit)sans prealablement auoir le cõgie
de lordinaire du lieu ou son cõmis a ce auec laduis ꝗ cõsentemt
de la faculte de theologie daucune Vniuersite prochaine approu
uant soubz le seau dicelle faculte lesditz liures ꝗ escriptures . Et

much against the holy orthodox faith and against that which the Catholic Apostolic Church has kept and observed to this day. We likewise condemn anything that speaks against the Holy Father, against the prelates of the church, and against the secular princes, the general schools and their faculties, and all other honest people, whether in positions of authority or not. And in the same manner we condemn everything that is contrary to the good moral character of the people, to the Holy Roman Church, and to the Christian public good.

And finally, after this edict has been published, we want all the books, writings, and pictures mentioned above to be publicly burned, including those under the name of any author that might be printed, written, or compiled in any language, wherever they may be found in our countries.

We ask you to be diligent in apprehending and confiscating all the belongings of those who seem rebellious to the ordinances herein mentioned and to punish them according to the penalties set out by law — divine, canon, and civil.

And so as to prevent poisonous false doctrines and bad examples from being spread all over Christendom, and so that the art of printing books might be used only toward good ends, we, after mature and long deliberation, order and command you by this edict that henceforth, under penalty of confiscation of goods and property, no book dealer, printer, or anybody else mention the Holy Scriptures or their interpretation without having first received the consent of the clerk of the city and the advice and consent of the faculty of theology of the university, which will approve those books and writings with their seal. As

---

Eutychian heresy was a form of monophysitism begun by Eutyches of Constantinople (d. *ca*. A.D. 454), who claimed that there were two natures in Christ before birth, but only one nature (the divine) after the Incarnation. Eutyches thus denied an individual and concrete existence for the human nature of Christ, since this was absorbed by his divinity.

quant aux aultres liures non traictans de la foy ou saincte es
cripture Voulons ce present decret pareillemēt estre garde. sauff
quil souffira auoir le congie de nous ou de noz lieutenans . Et
ce pour la premiere impression des dessusditz liures. ¶ Item de
clairons au surplus par ces dictes presentes q̃ si aucun de quelq̃
dignite degre ou cōdition quil soit presume ou est si ose hardy
ou temeraire de cōtreuenir a cestuy nostre p̃sent edit decret sta
tu loy ꝗ ordōnance directement ou indirectemēt tāt en ce qui cō
cerne le dessusdit dāne affaire de Luther ꝗ liures diffamatoires
ꝗ de limpression cy deuant dicte oultre ce q̃ nous irritons ꝗ anul
lons tout ce q̃ sera fait. lesditz transgresseurs en ce faisant ens
courront crime de lese maieste ꝗ nostre tresgriefue indignation
ꝗ toutes ꝗ chascunes les peines dessusdictes. ¶ Et pource que
de cestuy nostre present edit lon pourra auoir affaire en diuers
lieux nous Voulōs que aux copies escriptes ou imprimees col
latiōnees ꝗ signees par lung de noz secretaires ou par aucuns
notaires apostoliques foy soit adioustee cōme a ce present ori
ginal. ¶ En tesmoing de ce ꝗ a ce que ce soit chose ferme ꝗ esta
ble a tousiours nous auons fait mettre aux presentes nostre
grant seel ꝗ icelles signees de nostre main. ¶ Dōne en nostre
cite de VVormes le. viii. iour de May. Lan de grace Mil cinq
cens. xxi.

                    Ainsi signe   Charles

                                         Lalemand.

for books that do not even mention faith or the Holy Scriptures, we also want this decree applied to them, except that our consent or that of our lieutenants will be sufficient. All this will apply for the first printing of the books hereabove mentioned.

Item. Furthermore, we declare in this ordinance that if anyone, whatever his social status may be, dares directly or indirectly to oppose this decree — whether concerning Luther's matter, his defamatory books or their printings, or whatever has been ordered by us — these transgressors in so doing will be guilty of the crime of *lèse majesté* and will incur our grave indignation as well as each of the punishments mentioned above.

We desire that evidence be added to the copy of this decree, [namely, that it be] signed by one of our secretaries or by an apostolic notary as would be done for this original.

As a witness to this, and for all these things to be firm and forever established, we have put our seal on this document and have signed by our hand.

Given in our city of Worms on the eighth day of May in the year of our Lord one thousand five hundred twenty-one.

    Signed   Charles of Germany

Acknowledgments

I wish to express appreciation to the many people who have contributed in one way or another to this book. Meriting particular attention are Mr. Hugo Corstius, of Nijhoff's in The Hague, for furnishing us this copy of the edict and for assisting in the search for other editions; Mr. Ivan Volkoff for valuable recommendations on picture locations and for reading the manuscript in its early stages, offering several constructive suggestions; Michael Anderson and Robert Pusey for their help in various ways; Miss Jacquelin Delbrouwire for her assistance in translating the edict, and Dr. Keith Slade of the French Department for his suggestions that have improved the translation. Most appreciated is the constant support of Mr. Dean Larsen of the BYU Library, through whose efforts the edict was acquired in the first place and who suggested the project to me. I also appreciate the many months of patient editorial work contributed by Mr. John Drayton of the BYU Press.

DJ

PICTURE CREDITS

Cover — Zentralbibliothek, Zurich.

Pages ii, 10 (lower), 13, 14, 15, 26, 33, 45, 53, 61, 63, 67, 81, 97 — Lutherhalle, Wittenberg.

4 — Courtesy Foundation for Reformation Research, St. Louis.

7, 18, 19, 105 — Rare Books and Manuscripts Collection, Brigham Young University, Provo.

10 (upper) — *Propyläen Weltgeschichte,* vol. 5 (Berlin: Propyläen Verlag, 1930-32).

12 — Courtesy Metropolitan Museum of Art, New York, Fletcher Fund, 1919.

17 (upper) — Fortress Press, Philadelphia.

17 (lower), 22, 47, 49, 91 — Hamburger Kunsthalle, Hamburg.

20, 23, 32, 35, 51, 64 — Pflugk-Harttung, *Im Morgenrot der*

Reformation (Basel: Verlagsbuchhandlung A. Rohde, 1922).

21 — Internationale Bildagentur Oberengstringen, Zurich.

27, 68 — Siedlitz, *Allgemeines Historisches Porträtwerk* (Munich: Friedrich Bruckmann, 1894).

28, 38 — Germanisches Nationalmuseum, Nuremberg.

29, 34, 101 — Kaulfuss-Diesch, *Das Buch der Reformation* R. Voigtländer Verlag, 1917).

30, 31 — Schredkenbach & Neubert, *Martin Luther: Ein Bild seines Lebens und Wirkens* (Leipzig: Verlagsbuchhandlung von J. Weber, 1918).

41, 59, 60 — Stadtarchiv, Worms.

42 — Kupferstichkabinett, Berlin.

48 — Musée du Louvre, Paris.

52 — Courtesy University of Michigan Library, Ann Arbor.

54-55 — Staatsgalerie, Stuttgart.

56 — Courtesy Museum of Fine Arts, Boston.

58 — Public Record Office, London.

89 — Rosgartenmuseum, Konstanz.

Index

115

117